Luca Carrera

The Beautiful Game: How Brazil Changed Soccer Forever

The Beautiful Game: How Brazil Changed Soccer Forever

"The ball is made of leather, but in Brazil, it is stitched with dreams."
—Anonymous

Table of Contents

Chapter 1 Coffee Barons and British Pioneers: The Ball Arrives in Rio

The Royal Mail Steam Packet MAGDALENA nosed into Guanabara Bay on an April dawn thick with the smell of burned coffee husks. Dockside cranes creaked like waking gulls, and the launchmen shouted in English, Portuguese, and the clipped Yoruba of the stevedores who stacked burlap sacks for the barons of São Paulo's hinterland. Somewhere in her hold, jammed between crates of Sheffield cutlery and barrels of Manchester dye, lay a coarse linen parcel labeled ATHLETIC EQUIPMENT — HANDLE WITH CARE. Inside were four regulation footballs, stitched from twelve panels of Scottish cowhide and inflated on the voyage by a curious cabin boy who had never seen their like.

Nobody paid the parcel much mind that morning—certainly not the customs officer who damp-stamped cargo manifests while plotting his afternoon caipirinha. In a ledger entry dated 18 April 1886, the equipment is lumped together with "miscellany for private club use," a bureaucratic shrug at what would become the fuse for an explosion of Brazilian culture. Yet in hindsight the moment feels electric, like the crack of flint to tinder. Those balls were rolling toward destiny: toward samba rhythms, toward Pelé's volley in Stockholm, toward televisions glowing yellow across the planet.

Clubs of Empire and Coffee

If Rio at the fin de siècle was a mosaic, the brightest tiles were British. The Empire's merchants had trailed rail lines and insatiable coffee contracts deep into Brazil's interior, and every few months they returned to the capital in search of cool sea breezes and a taste of home. They brought with them not only the King's English but the King's games—cricket bats, tennis rackets, and, increasingly, the latest craze gripping industrial northern England: association football.

The community's redoubt was the Rio Cricket Club, founded in 1872 by a pair of shipping agents named Basil Freeland and George Emmanuel Cox. They leased a dusty plot in Botafogo, then a sleepy suburb where mangrove trees dipped into an iridescent lagoon. Box-hedge boundaries and a tin-roofed pavilion lent the ground an Edwardian dignity that must have looked other-worldly to carioca fishermen poling their canoes past. By 1897, the club had migrated across the bay to Niterói—renaming itself Rio Cricket & Athletic Association—largely because the original pitch flooded at high tide and because its members craved more space for new diversions, chief among them football. Carioca Cricket Club

On Sunday afternoons, after a polite lunch of roast beef and mango chutney, the bankers and insurance clerks removed straw boaters, rolled up shirt-sleeves, and kicked leather spheres across the baked earth. They played halves of twenty minutes—any longer invited heatstroke—and adhered to a strict code: no dribbling more than ten paces, no sliding in the dust that scuffed linen trousers, and absolutely no locals unless vouched for by a paying member. The lone spectator most days was a goat tethered by the boundary rope, indifferent to origin stories.

Yet word leaked beyond the picket fence. Carioca boys peered through knot-holes, memorizing the trajectories of toe-poked passes, and one bold teen named João de Souza allegedly sneaked onto the grounds at midnight to trace the pitch dimensions with a lantern so he could chalk an imitation field behind the fishermen's chapel. Thirty years later, Souza's grandson would sign professional forms for Fluminense. History, here, runs on braids of coincidence.

Oscar and the Oarsmen

Fluminense itself owes existence to an Anglo-Brazilian daydreamer with an oar in one hand and a business ledger in the other. Oscar Cox was the son of a wealthy shipping executive who divided his adolescence between rowing on the Thames and rowing on the Rio lagoon. In 1901 he traveled to Switzerland on holiday, fell in with Geneva schoolboys besotted by football, and returned to Brazil with a conviction that rowing clubs were yesterday's fashion. Cox proselytized with missionary fervor, buttonholing his father's associates at the Paissandu Athletic Club bar and predicting that soon every respectable gentleman in Rio would swap oarlocks for goalposts.

A year later, on 21 July 1902, in the drawing room of the Clube de Xadrez in Laranjeiras, Cox and nineteen colleagues founded Fluminense Football Club—the first Brazilian side to enshrine the word "football" in its legal title. They elected English-born Horácio da Costa Santos president and adopted cherry, white, and bottle-green kits that resembled the striped waistcoats of Savile Row racegoers. Cox personally ordered a fresh consignment of balls from Mitre's Leeds factory, along with rule books and crossbars, for the princely sum of 32 pounds sterling. FIFA

Fluminense's inaugural public match came against Rio Cricket in October 1903. The novelty drew carriages three-deep along Rua Álvaro Chaves and a sprinkling of society ladies in Parisian parasols who asked whether the leather orb might burst if struck too hard. Cox, captaining the hosts, scored the first goal after sixteen minutes—a scuffed effort that trickled under the goalkeeper's boot. The JORNAL DO COMÉRCIO described the crowd's reaction as "a restrained ripple of applause befitting an operetta encore," but one awestruck spectator recalled something wilder: "When the ball crossed the line we felt a shock of electricity, as if the city's axis swung a degree." That eyewitness, Augusto Brandão, would later help found Botafogo.

The Coffee Factor

Money flowed in the background like dark roast syrup. Brazil's coffee boom of the 1890s had minted an industrial aristocracy eager to ape European leisure pursuits. The same barons who funded opera houses and cattle auctions now underwrote football pitches, wagering that sporting success could launder provincial roughness into cosmopolitan polish. São Paulo plantation scion Antônio Prado financed the expansion of the São Paulo Athletic Club, enabling Charles Miller's fledgling league to import referees from Southampton. In Rio, exporters like Francisco Guinle donated turf seed, iron fencing, and even lime for touchlines, all in anticipation of champagne receptions beneath grandstands that had not yet been built.

Behind the patronage lay politics. Brazil's 1889 switch from empire to republic produced an elite anxious to prove modernity on par with London or Paris. Football, codified in English boarding schools and spreading across continental capitals, offered a low-risk, high-visibility badge of progress. A visiting Yorkshire engineer, Reginald Firth, wrote to his sister in 1898: "These planter fellows can barely string a telegraph line between estates, yet they'll kick this ball as if civilization itself depends upon it." He was only half-joking.

The Scottish Textile Men

Not every pioneer wore a monocle. Seventy kilometers inland, in the textile district of Bangu, a Scottish loom mechanic named Thomas Donohoe was teaching factory laborers to dribble in hobnailed boots during Sunday picnics beneath jacaranda trees. Donohoe had arrived in 1894 to service steam looms but discovered none of his colleagues had heard of football. So he wrote to his wife in Kirkintilloch for a ball, patched together a team of machinists and dyers, and staged informal matches on scrub ground behind the warehouse.

Local lore claims these were the first games in Rio state to feature working-class Brazilians rather than British expats. When Donohoe and his mates petitioned the mill owners for official recognition, they were rebuffed—management preferred brass bands to sweaty scrimmages—but persistence won out. On 7 April 1904, Bangu Athletic Club was born, notable as the first Brazilian side to open membership to black and mixed-race players. WikipediaScottish Football MuseumRoyal Gazette

Their kit—white shirts with a red sash—was sewn from off-cut factory cotton, and Donohoe insisted everyone pay equal dues. "On the pitch we are comrades, not overseers," he was quoted in the GAZETA DE NOTÍCIAS. That egalitarian credo foreshadowed seismic battles over race and class that would soon convulse Brazilian sport.

A Ballad of Dust and Decorum

While Bangu's apprentices slogged through muddy apprenticeships, the high society set in Rio polished its manners to Victorian sheen. Matches at Paissandu or Rio Cricket began with a formal bow to the pavilion and ended with gin-and-tonic toasts under punkah fans. Goal scorers were expected to tip caps to the bandstand and shake hands with the goalkeeper they had just humiliated. One British consul joked that the only serious foul in those days was perspiring on a silk waistcoat.

Yet collisions—both physical and social—proved inevitable. In June 1905, during a friendly between Fluminense and Rio

Cricket, a Carioca forward named Alberto Borgerth slid in studs-up on visiting half-back Herbert Schofield. Dust and insults clouded the air. The CORREIO DA MANHÃ labeled the incident "a regrettable eruption of continentale passions," but privately many spectators thrilled to the raw spectacle. It was as if football had shed its top hat for a carnival mask, promising something more voluptuous than polite recreation.

The alarmed British clubs responded by tightening eligibility. Minutes from a Rio Cricket committee meeting in September 1905 propose a rule limiting future membership to "gentlemen of demonstrated European birth or lineage." It was a doomed attempt to dam a surging tide. Within five years, mixed-race and working-class players would dominate local competitions, and the Anglo-Brazilian amateurs retreated to cricket nets where the old etiquette still reigned.

Charles Miller's Flying Visit

In December 1906, a lean mustachioed man in a tweed traveling suit stepped onto Rio's platform of the Estrada de Ferro Central. Charles William Miller had come from São Paulo to arrange an inter-city exhibition between his São Paulo Athletic Club (SPAC) and Fluminense, a contest newspaper editors were already hyping as the "Game of the Century" though the sport had existed here barely a decade. Miller was thirty-two, fluent in Portuguese, English, and the universal patois of changing rooms.

He met Oscar Cox in the lobby of the Grande Hotel to finalize rules: ninety-minute halves instead of forty-fives, a proper referee from Glasgow, and—Miller's insistence—an FA-sanctioned match ball shipped directly from Hampshire to avoid the "bladder irregularities" of local copies. The affair took place on 22 June 1907 at Laranjeiras under oppressive humidity. SPAC won 4–2, Miller scoring twice, but the real victory was aesthetic. A record 1,200 spectators attended, including a delegation of congressmen who filed motions the following week to develop public playing fields. Wikipedia

Miller wrote in a letter to an English friend: "If the politicians grasp this game's potency, they will harness it like a coffee mule. The people cannot resist its spell." Prophetic words.

Beyond the Picket Fence

By the turn of the century, balls were arriving not piecemeal in steamer trunks but by the crate. Sporting-goods importers sprang up along Rua do Ouvidor, advertising boots alongside fencing foils. A 1908 catalog from Casa Sportiva listed three models: MODELO INGLÊS DE COURO FINO (two milréis), MODELO ESCOLAR (one milréis), and the bargain BOLA POPULAR, stitched in nearby Petrópolis from goat hide so coarse it bruised ankles.

The technology gap between elite and street mattered less than one might think. On public squares, boys wrapped rags into spheres; on beaches they shaped wet sand; in tenements they chased oranges until the fruit burst. A young dock porter named João Coelho Neto—later the novelist

"Preguinho" and Brazil's first World Cup captain—learned by juggling papayas outside his mother's laundry. He swore the wobble of soft fruit trained his instep better than any imported leather.

A Fuse Ignites

In retrospect, the period from 1894 to 1910 resembles the timer on a carnival firework: a hiss of friction, a pause pregnant with sulfur, and then a blast of irrepressible color. Each British pioneer unwittingly handed off a glowing baton to a Brazilian counterpart who would sprint beyond the boundaries of class, race, and decorum. The coffee barons provided capital, but the masses supplied myth. As the twentieth century gathered speed, the sport began to tilt away from expatriate ownership and toward something profoundly Brazilian—chaotic, rhythmic, democratic.

Late one December twilight in 1909, a groundskeeper at Fluminense locked the pavilion and started home. In his diary—discovered a century later in a mildew-stained attic—he noted "three barefoot lads on the pitch practicing until darkness swallowed them." He had no heart to chase them off; the club had already scored its victory in the afternoon's fixture. "Let them play," he wrote. "The future is theirs, not ours."

He was right. Within a generation, those barefoot heirs would lace boots for clubs named Flamengo, Botafogo, America, Vasco, and eventually the Seleção itself. They would graft samba hips onto Victorian rules, lace the game with capoeira feints, and invite the world to watch. But that transformation begins with our next chapter, when a young rail engineer's son steps off a ship in Santos, clutching two footballs and a rulebook printed in blue ink.

The ball has arrived in Brazil; now it must find its voice.

Chapter 2   Charles Miller's Suitcase

The whistle of the inbound liner echoed off the warehouses of Santos like a shot in a cathedral. October 1894, rainy season just beginning, and a young man in an English tweed traveling suit leaned over the rail to smell the harbor's sharp mix of coffee husk, diesel, and Atlantic brine. Charles William Miller—twenty-year-old son of a Scottish railway engineer and a Brazilian mother of English descent—had been away from home for ten years, long enough for the cobblestones of São Paulo to shrink in memory, long enough to acquire that half-sardonic, half-self-possessed tilt of the head that English public schools used as finishing polish. Tucked under his arm were two deflated leather footballs wrapped in a linen shirt. In his suitcase sat a dog-eared booklet of Hampshire Football Association laws, a hand-pump, and a determination to transplant the game that had bewitched him on fog-slicked Saturdays in Southampton.

Dockhands barely noticed him. They were too busy coaxing bale after bale of green coffee toward open rail wagons destined for the Serra do Mar incline. Yet the seed of what Brazilians would one day call FUTEBOL-ARTE was stepping onto the gangplank, disguised as a polite young clerk returning from study abroad. Miller's first words on Brazilian soil were practical rather than prophetic: "Careful—that case is fragile." The porter shrugged; every immigrant claimed their baggage held treasure. In Miller's instance, it did.

He reached São Paulo three days later by narrow-gauge train, the Serra's cloudbanks parting to reveal jagged valleys where telegraph poles looked like matchsticks. At each whistle-stop, farmers hawked bananas through the windows, and Miller secretly wondered if any of them would one day juggle a football with the nonchalance he had seen displayed by Thames-side schoolboys. In the carriage opposite him, a railway accountant read the GAZETA DE NOTÍCIAS. The headline spoke of political wrangling in Rio, but the sub-head caught Miller's eye: "City Clubs Seek Modern Recreations." He smiled. Timing, it seemed, was marching in step with him.

Home in the Brás district, the reunion was warm but brief; the São Paulo Railway Company expected him at his desk by Monday. Yet even before he located his inkwell, Miller was plotting. He inflated one ball behind the company workshop, hammered four wooden stakes into an idle freight yard, and after the afternoon whistle invited a handful of clerks and mechanics to "try an English pastime." They lined up in braces and scuffed boots, laughing at the oddity. The first attempted kick sent the ball skidding under a water cart, but within minutes instinct overrode awkwardness and the men were chasing, tackling, celebrating as if rules were secondary to revelation. Overtime on the ledgers would wait; something more urgent had arrived.

Word spread faster than steam could carry it. On Sundays, the railway yard hosted impromptu matches that drew curious stares from passers-by. Not all observers approved. A priest complained that grown men sprinting in shirtsleeves on the Lord's Day resembled "dockyard dogs fighting over offal." Yet the momentum was irreversible. São Paulo's British expatriate enclave, already clustered around the São

Paulo Athletic Club (SPAC) for cricket and rugby, sensed a new sporting current. At Miller's urging, SPAC ordered additional balls from a firm in Sheffield and set aside a sloping corner of the Pirituba field for football practice. The slope stayed; early matches required defying geography as well as defenders.

Miller insisted on discipline. He chalk-lined a regulation 100 × 50-yard pitch, lectured teammates on the offside trap, and placed goalkeepers in woolen sweaters despite tropical heat because that was how it was done on the Solent. He introduced the 2-3-5 "pyramid" formation, with himself orchestrating play at centre-forward, barking commands in a hybrid accent that mashed Portuguese vowels with Hampshire consonants. "Passa—agora—inside!" he would yell, stunning opponents who had yet to categorize the positions he referenced.

The first formal contest took place on 14 April 1895: São Paulo Railway Company versus employees of the São Paulo Gas Company, assembled on a rough field at Várzea do Carmo near the Tietê River. Spectators arrived out of curiosity rather than allegiance, some perching on carts, others dangling legs from a culvert. The kickoff produced cheers, laughter, and occasional jeers whenever a player tripped on anthills. Miller scored twice, naturally, guiding the railway men to a 4–2 victory. More important than the score was the sight: linen shirts splashed with red mud, a whistle's shrill authority, and a spellbinding object that never left the ground for more than a few heartbeats before someone killed it with a boot. Witnesses later swore they felt the city tilt that day, as if its clockwork had discovered a new rhythm.

Within months, matches multiplied. Bank clerks challenged postal workers; the light-blue of SPAC squared off against a hastily assembled team of German technicians from the Jafet textile mill. In lieu of proper goal nets, players stretched fishing slings between posts or left goals open, policing honesty through shouted consensus. Boot laces snapped; players borrowed rope. One afternoon's downpour turned the pitch into chocolate pudding, but both sides played on, attracting street children who squealed whenever a slide tackle sent mud spraying like carnival confetti.

Miller's office hours blurred with his evangelism. He wrote circulars to English friends, pleading for jerseys, boots, and more balls—"quality leather if you can manage it; these local goatskins rupture disgracefully." He also petitioned São Paulo's municipal elders to allocate flat public land, arguing that football promoted "discipline, hygiene, and civic morale." The city fathers, chafing under British influence yet hungry for modernity, granted him a modest rectangle near the Luz station on condition he maintain fencing and keep play to daylight.

Meanwhile, the São Paulo elite watched from verandas. Coffee barons who fancied themselves arbiters of fashion grew intrigued. Their sons, schooled in Paris, returned with gossip that football matches in London drew crowds of twenty thousand. Could such spectacle elevate São Paulo's status? Eager to outshine rival Rio, magnates funded pavilion repairs at SPAC and laid a cinder track for spectators in top hats. When Miller proposed an inter-city exhibition against Fluminense in Rio, the planters secretly wagered on their own city's superiority, underwriting rail tickets and a brass band.

That first Paulista-Carioca showdown in 1901 was less a game than a summit. Miller, impeccably groomed, captained SPAC. Opposite him stood Oscar Cox, the suave Anglo-Brazilian founder of Fluminense whom Miller had met years earlier in Southampton's boarding-house stairwells. The two hugged, posed for newspaper sketches, and promptly turned adversaries when the whistle blew. SPAC won 2–1, but Rio's defenders admitted they had never seen passing triangles executed with such geometry. Cox invited Miller to dinner the next evening, and between glasses of claret they mapped out a dream: a national championship, traveling between capitals, forging a sporting identity larger than any one city. Bureaucracy would stall that ambition for decades, but the seed-planting felt revolutionary.

Back in São Paulo, Miller moved quickly. He convinced four local clubs—SPAC, Mackenzie College, Clube Atlético Paulistano, and Internacional-SP—to establish the Liga Paulista de Foot-Ball, Brazil's first structured league. The 1902 season opened under low rainclouds but drew an audience of 1,500 to SPAC's ground, a figure that astonished newspaper editors who had assumed football was a passing British fad. By season's end, SPAC were champions, Miller the top scorer, and children across the city were rolling oranges in alleyways pretending to be "Charlie Miller" finishing at the near post.

Tactically, Miller's most significant contribution was evangelizing positional play. He drilled full-backs to remain staggered rather than chase the ball, urged half-backs to funnel possession through inside-forwards, and treated the centre-forward role as both spearhead and decoy. Observers accustomed to rugby's straight-line charges dubbed his patterns "the spiderweb." Rivals copied him. Thus São Paulo became Brazil's first laboratory for systematic football thinking, producing early disciples who would later carry lessons to Rio, Belo Horizonte, and Porto Alegre.

Yet accolades never swelled his ego into tyranny. Teammates recalled that between halves he passed around oranges and cracked jokes about how English rain trained him for Brazilian drizzle. He refused honorary club privileges, preferring to wash mud off boots alongside groundskeepers. His most radical principle was inclusivity—limited, in those first years, by prevailing racial hierarchies but still open enough to allow skilled clerks of modest means into SPAC's lineup. The move scandalized certain planters who believed sport should mirror society's class partitions. Miller countered that ability, not aristocracy, should select a footballer. It was a polite argument—he remained every inch the Victorian gentleman—but its implications undermined pillars of social order.

Inevitably, there were setbacks. The 1906 season ended with SPAC's humiliating 9–1 defeat by Internacional-SP, a rout that exposed their reliance on aging core players and hinted at how quickly Brazilian clubs were mastering the imported craft. Miller, playing goalkeeper that day due to injuries in the squad, endured the onslaught stoically, then offered his resignation from the league's board, claiming fresh leadership was necessary. He remained a player but ceded administrative control, an act that accelerated the league's democratization as locals filled committee seats formerly reserved for British expatriates.

Miller's later years drifted from the limelight. He married the celebrated pianist Antonietta Rudge, fathered two children, invested in suburban real-estate developments, and served briefly as Acting British Vice-Consul. Friends noted he attended matches less often, content to smoke his pipe near the touchline and critique volleys with a raised eyebrow. But the architecture he erected—leagues, rivalries, a belief that Brazil could host football on equal footing with Europe—stood intact. When São Paulo's Corinthians club was baptized in 1910, inspired by the English amateur side he once faced, Miller lent moral support, if not finances, acknowledging that the game's ownership had passed to new custodians.

One rainy afternoon in 1926, a journalist asked the now-graying pioneer if he regretted surrendering center stage. Miller shook his head. "I merely carried the seed," he said. "Brazil provided the sunlight, the soil, and the carnival music." He gestured toward a nearby vacant lot where barefoot youths were dribbling a rag ball between puddles. "Look," he whispered, "they don't need an English gardener anymore."

Decades later, scholars would position Miller as the hinge between British order and Brazilian improvisation—the moment the rulebook met the rumba. Without his suitcase full of leather and laws there might still have been a game, but it would have arrived slower, perhaps shaped by other hands, less attuned to tactical nuance. His genius lay not in inventing football, nor in perfecting it, but in recognizing that São Paulo's restless energy could ignite the sport into something the mother country never imagined: a swirling, samba-tinged spectacle that would one day bring Scandinavian crowds to their feet and force tactical revolutions on Europe's grandest stages.

When Miller died in 1953, obituaries in England gave him two paragraphs. Brazilian papers devoted entire pages, framing him alongside coffee, samba, and the Amazon as one of the nation's transformative conduits. Among the tributes, a note from an anonymous fan arrived at SPAC's shuttered football pavilion. It read: OBRIGADO POR ACENDER A CHAMA – THANK YOU FOR STRIKING THE MATCH.

The match, once struck, would burn through another century, through Pelé's bicycle-kick silhouette and Marta's victorious grin, through World Cup ecstasies and Olympic redemptions. But every flame has a spark, and in Brazil that first spark was the hiss of a steamship, the creak of a gangplank, and a young man steadying a suitcase against the bustle of Santos harbor.

Chapter 3   From Mansions to Morros: Football Leaves the Garden Gates

The year was 1906, and Rio de Janeiro's social map could be traced by the whiff of leisure each neighborhood exhaled. In the manicured gardens of Laranjeiras, young aristocrats in linen whites rehearsed polite passes beneath a jacaranda's purple bloom, their mothers applauding from cane chairs. Ten miles north, in the furnace-red factory district of Bangu, a steam whistle marked quitting time and a different tribe spilled onto a cinder lot hemmed in by brick chimneys. They wore burlap shorts, bled dye from the textile vats, and played with a scuffed ball sewn from factory off-cuts. When Fluminense's dapper first eleven agreed to cross the city for a "friendly" against Bangu Athletic Club, the GAZETA DE NOTÍCIAS dubbed it O ENCONTRO DE DOIS MUNDOS—the meeting of two worlds.

What unfolded was less a football match than a social thunderclap. Bangu's inside-left, Francisco Carregal—one of the first black Brazilians to lace up in an organized contest— ghosted past Fluminense's starched defenders with a repertoire of swivels the Rio elite had never seen. Spectators gasped, not merely at the scoreline (a 4–0 shock for the home side) but at the upheaval of etiquette: bare feet celebrated beside patent-leather brogues, mulatto factory hands outwitted scions of coffee dynasties. By sundown, well-heeled visitors were hurrying back to their carriages, confused by the joy that had rattled their class compass. The ball, once a garden ornament of the privileged, had vaulted the picket fence.

The Birth of PELADA: Improvisation as Pedagogy

As the sport seeped into Rio's working-class arteries, formal kit proved optional. Children in Gamboa juggled oranges until the fruit burst; stevedores in Saúde tied rags around bull-bladder bladders to create a misshapen sphere they called PELADA—literally "naked," stripped of pomp. With rules negotiated on the fly, goals were two stones or a pair of sandals, and any patch of earth wide enough for ten strides became Wembley. PELADA taught economy of motion: a heavy rag ball died quickly on the bounce, so the first touch had to be velvet, the second touch lethal. Off-balance creativity became muscle memory; later, when these boys encountered regulation leather, it felt buoyant as helium.

A legend survives from Morro da Providência—Brazil's first favela, carved by Canudos War veterans atop a granite hump overlooking the port. One twilight in 1908, a teenage dock porter named Otávio dos Santos watched an inbound steamer unload crates stenciled "FOOT-BALLS." Unable to afford one, he and his friends spent a month braiding banana leaves into a tight oval and coated it with paraffin for bounce. They practiced dribbles on the hill's crooked stairways, where keeping the ball from tumbling into the alley below honed a preternatural close control. Otávio never played professionally; he became a trolley conductor. But two decades later, his youngest brother Germano—raised on the same stair-dribble discipline—joined America FC and introduced a move teammates called O DEGRAU INVISÍVEL, the invisible step, a stutter-feint that left full-backs grasping air.

Liga Suburbana de Football: Democracy on a Dust Bowl

Improvisation soon demanded structure. In April 1907, eight self-financed neighborhood clubs convened in a rented hall on Rua Minas, Sampaio, to found the Liga Suburbana de Football. The minutes of that smoky meeting reveal young men in coveralls debating fixture lists with the solemnity of diplomats. Their playing field in Riachuelo was a dust bowl littered with tram-line cinders; spectators stood behind a rope strung between trolley poles; the prize was a tin cup purchased by passing the hat at a Saturday CHURRASCO. Yet the league's impact was seismic: for the first time, black sailors marked white bookkeepers in sanctioned competition, and stovemakers from Riachuelo hurled taunts at telegraph clerks from Engenho Novo—all under the same referee's whistle.

Riachuelo FC won that inaugural season, thanks largely to a goalkeeper nicknamed "Palhaço" (the Clown) for his habit of flipping into handstands after each save. Reporters dismissed the gesture as uncouth, but children copied it in street games, discovering that showmanship could distract a penalty taker as effectively as a fingertip. Thus tricks filtered upward: by 1913, Fluminense's reserve keeper was practicing Palhaço's cartwheels in private, wary of purist backlash yet hungry for any edge.

Bangu's Red-and-White Rebellion

Across the city, Bangu Athletic Club evolved into a laboratory of working-class audacity. Scottish foreman Thomas Donohoe had opened membership to factory laborers in 1904, and within two seasons the roster resembled the dye works night shift: Portuguese loom mechanics, Afro-Brazilian pressers, and mulatto boys who reeked of indigo. Management disapproved—sport, they felt, should civilize not radicalize—but goals trumped hierarchy. When Bangu entered the 1906 Campeonato Carioca against Fluminense and Botafogo's gentleman amateurs, journalists sneered that the "dyers" would wilt in polite company. They did not: Bangu finished third, and Carregal's rainbow flick over a Fluminense half-back was replayed in café gossip for weeks.

The real revolution lay off the pitch. After Saturday matches, Bangu players staged SAMBA DE RODA parties where factory foremen clinked beer mugs with mill hands under a single string of lanterns. In a stratified empire still tasting the ash of slavery (abolished only eighteen years earlier), that communal swirl felt dangerous. Municipal police filed reports on "rowdy gatherings" but could not legislate the chemistry of celebration. Football had done in ninety minutes what abolition and the republic's constitution had failed to achieve in decades: it put calloused and manicured palms on the same trophy.

Morro Voices, Mansion Ears

Meanwhile, from the MORROS—Providência, Mangueira, Santo Antônio—new sounds drifted downhill. Youngsters hammered cooking pots into drums and invented chants to accompany pick-up matches. One ditty began, "NOSSA BOLA É DE PANO, MAS VOA COMO AVIÃO"—our ball is cloth, but it flies like an airplane—a brag that reached Laranjeiras terraces via laundresses who washed for Fluminense households. On match days, some elite spectators found themselves humming favela choruses they pretended not to recognize. Music, like the ball, proved porous.

Even the tactics evolved in this cross-pollination. Mansion-bred players favored crisp, straight-line passing—echoes of Edwardian cricket. Hill players, constrained by uneven ground, learned to swerve around potholes, using hips to mask direction changes. When mixed-class friendlies became common around 1910, Fluminense's defenders complained that MENINOS DO MORRO dribbled in "curved spells," twisting ankles on pristine grass but leaving markers dizzy. Coach Harry Welfare—an English striker turned manager—took notes. Soon Fluminense experimented with wider forward lines to counter the serpentine runs. Thus the favela's topography re-etched the city's premier formation board.

Football Meets the Tramline

Transportation accelerated the blend. In 1908 the Rio Tram Company completed an electric line snaking from Carioca station to the seaward suburbs. Suddenly a mill worker from São Cristóvão could ride for one tostão to a beachside PELADA, then hop back for the night shift. The ball rolled wherever rails glinted. Stories multiply of impromptu matches at terminus loops, conductors timing kick-abouts between scheduled departures. A conductor named Sebastião once delayed a tram to finish a hat-trick; his passengers cheered instead of complaining, and the incident made O PAIZ under the headline "The Tram That Scored a Goal."

A Glimpse of 1923: Shadows of Resistance

By the early 1920s the talent pipeline from hilltops to stadiums was undeniable, but the establishment pushed back. When Vasco da Gama's multi-racial, dockworker-heavy squad stormed the 1923 Campeonato Carioca, rival clubs demanded a new, "more selective" league that would bar Vasco's black and working-class stars. Vasco refused, publishing the now-famous RESPOSTA HISTÓRICA—a 2,000-word rebuke that listed every ostracized player by name and refused to trade inclusion for prestige. The letter electrified the suburbs; teenage players pinned clippings above their hammocks as proof that a rag-ball dream might yet conquer the marble pavilions.

The Creative Dividend

With barriers crumbling, improvisation became currency. A 1924 PELADA on the sand flats of Praça Onze produced the first recorded ELÁSTICO—a rubber-band feint later popularized by Rivellino half a century on. The inventor, a baker's apprentice nicknamed "Cebola," never earned a professional contract, but Fluminense winger Alfredinho witnessed the trick and replicated it in a league match the following season. Observers declared the move "pure Carioca malandragem"—rascalry transfigured into art.

Coaches faced a dilemma: how to codify a style born of scarcity without suffocating its spontaneity. Some tried numerical drills; others organized night-time scrimmages under gas lamps so players from factories could attend after hours. None captured the phenomenon fully, because PELADA remained a living classroom, adaptable, unaffiliated, prone to vanish when authorities fenced a vacant lot or when police chased gamblers from sidewalk corner goals. Yet like wildflowers, it sprouted elsewhere, each transplant mutating the genes of Brazilian football a shade brighter.

Sunset Over the Viaduto

On a hazy March evening in 1925, an amateur final of the Liga Suburbana drew 5,000 spectators to a weedy field beneath the Santa Teresa viaduct. Vendors sold black-bean stew from tin cans; a single phonograph blasted SAMBA-CANÇÃO into the dusk. When Riachuelo FC lifted the tin cup, their captain—a postal clerk—raised it toward the sky as electric trams rattled overhead carrying home opera-goers in tails and gowns. Two audiences, two worlds, one soundtrack of whistles and drum taps. By then, no commentator could pretend the sport belonged to the mansions alone; the morros had claimed equal authorship.

In less than a generation, football's center of gravity had slid downhill and uptown simultaneously, mingling dance steps with duty rosters, turning the city itself into a single sprawling stadium. The garden gates stood ajar, and through them poured rhythms, slang, and tactical heresies that would, in time, enthrall the globe. The next chapter will follow the club that weaponized that fusion—Vasco da Gama—and the seismic 1923 season that forced Brazil to confront the long-ignored question of race on the pitch. But first, pause on the viaduct's parapet as twilight fades: somewhere below, on a lamp-lit stairway, a boy chases a cloth ball that slips his toe and sails into night. By the time it lands, the game will belong to everyone.

Chapter 4 Black Boots on White Lines: Vasco da Gama and the 1923 Uprising

The final whistle on Rua Paissandu exploded like a starter's pistol for history. On the afternoon of 26 August 1923, eleven men in soot-black jerseys—work-worn wrists taped, laces frayed, boots polished only by the dust—collapsed into one another as the scoreboard confirmed the impossible: Vasco da Gama, the dockworkers' club from the unfashionable North Zone, were champions of Rio de Janeiro. Carioca high society, fanning itself behind parasols, stared at the rectangle of white chalk where hierarchy had just been redrawn. A sport imported to showcase elegance now blared a new anthem: rhythm, resilience, revolt.

The press rushed to label them **Os Camisas Negras**, the Black Shirts, but race, class, and kit color were inseparable. José Paschoal, a stevedore who could trap a ball with the hush of silk, lined up beside Bolão, the shoemaker's son who learned headers by nodding laundry bundles onto shelves. Their centre-half, Nicolino, kept time like a factory punch clock; their inside-left, Cecy, dribbled as if the ball were late for carnival. Ten of the squad were black or mixed-race, eight were blue-collar laborers, not one owned the patent-leather boots fashionable in Flamengo's dressing room. They wore the scuffs like medals.

What shocked polite Rio was not simply that Vasco won—it was how. They topped both rounds of the **Campeonato Carioca**, beating aristocratic flag-bearers América, Botafogo, and Fluminense on the trot. Reporters accustomed to stately 2–1 scorelines watched Vasco's forwards tear through defensive cordons with **malandragem** feints honed on cobblestones. After a 3–0 jolting of Fluminense, O JORNAL sniffed that the victors displayed "unnecessary exuberance." The next morning, kids on the tram to Praça Onze were already mimicking Cecy's flick-behind-the-heel, unnecessary or not.

Behind the rickety grandstands, the triumph felt cosmic. Longshoremen at the Cais do Porto danced a circle samba around an upturned barrel; seamstresses in Andaraí chalked goalposts on an alley wall for an after-shift kick-about; the Morro da Mangueira school band rewrote its opening march to include the chant **"Ninguém segura o Vasco!"**—nobody stops Vasco. The club's small ground in São Cristóvão became a pilgrimage site; supporters queued to touch the splintered corner flag as if holiness might rub off.

Yet every wave invites undertow. Off the pitch, Rio's sporting establishment tore pages from the rulebook searching for leverage. In October a cabal of elite clubs convened at the aristocratic Cassino Fluminense, sipping iced French vermouth while lamenting the erosion of DECORO ESPORTIVO— sporting decorum. Their solution was bureaucratic sleight of hand: dissolve the egalitarian **Liga Metropolitana de Desportos Terrestres** and form a new, invitation-only federation, the **Associação Metropolitana de Esportes Athleticos (AMEA)**. Entry would require "adequate sporting facilities" and, crucially, players with "proved means of subsistence and moral standing." It was a velvet-gloved color bar: twelve of Vasco's starters—dockers, typographers, car-washers—failed the test.

On 2 February 1924, AMEA's secretary delivered an ultimatum: ban the twelve "undesirables" or forfeit membership in the new league. The missive landed on the mahogany desk of Vasco president **José Augusto Prestes**, a grocer's son who had spent childhood dawns unloading sardine crates. He read it twice, poured a demitasse of thick coffee, and began writing the reply that would ricochet far beyond sport.

The document, **"A Resposta Histórica,"** ran four single-spaced pages and named each threatened player— **Brilhante, Defensor, Bolão, Nicolino, Paschoal, ...**—like saints in a litany. "We would rather lose honors than betray our athletes," Prestes wrote. "If we must choose between a championship and dignity, we choose dignity." He slid the letter into an envelope bearing the club's compass-rose seal and dispatched it by hand to AMEA headquarters, then walked across the courtyard to tell the team. Several players wept; Cecy muttered, "We win on the field, they fight in the boardroom."

AMEA's reply was silence. Vasco were out. For the 1924 season they played a patchwork calendar against minor teams left in the old league—Estácio, Bonsucesso, Vila Isabel—drawing bigger crowds than ever. Street vendors sold **"Resposta Histórica"** broadsheets alongside peanuts and matchbooks; barbers framed the letter by their mirrors. Carnival that year erupted into a call-and-response: one bloco shouting "Doze jogadores!" and another answering

"Uma só camisa!"—twelve players, one shirt.

Resistance spilled into court. Civil-rights lawyer Evaristo de Almeida filed an injunction arguing that public grounds could not host racially exclusive competitions. The case stalled in labyrinthine appeals, but the hearings produced unforgettable theater: Nicolino testifying in muddy boots after a friendly; a Botafogo director insisting under oath that "football demands social refinement." Newspapers ran verbatim courtroom clashes; in Carioca cafés, patrons replayed dialogue like radio soap operas.

AMEA's fortress cracked under its own contradictions. Flamengo discovered that sponsorship waned without Vasco derbies; Fluminense's gate receipts dipped, and season-ticket holders muttered about dull scorelines. By mid-1925, pragmatism trumped prejudice. Under a face-saving agreement, AMEA readmitted Vasco on condition they build a bigger stadium—an engineering hurdle the club embraced with gusto. Volunteers dug foundations by lamplight; Portuguese masons laid terraces in exchange for lifetime passes; women's circles organized bake sales to pay for cement. In April 1927 the **Estádio Vasco da Gama**, popularly the **São Januário**, opened with 40,000 roaring patrons and banners that proclaimed **"Aqui o negro e o branco jogam de mãos dadas"**—here, black and white play hand in hand.

From that terrace, ripples widened. Flamengo signed its first black forward within a year; Botafogo enlisted Leônidas da Silva, future inventor of the bicycle kick. By 1933, when Brazil legalized professionalism, rosters across the country looked more like dockyards than drawing rooms.

Much of Brazil's democratic myth-making around football would later fasten on Pelé, Garrincha, and Tele Santana's dreamers, but the crucible was 1923. Vasco's camisas negras did more than lift a trophy; they forced a closed society to redraw its sideline chalk, turning white lines into invitation lines. Their boots, dipped in factory dust, trampled a century of segregationist etiquette, proving that beauty could rise from sweat as surely as from silk.

On match days now, when the São Januário PA system crackles alive, a recording of Prestes's closing words from the Resposta Histórica plays over the loudspeakers: **"Nenhum título vale a indignidade."** No title is worth indignity. The stadium lights bloom, the drums strike up, and players of every hue jog onto the green—proof that a letter, a stand, and a season of uprising can echo for a hundred years.

Chapter 5 Leônidas and the Birth of the Bicycle Kick

Paris, 5 June 1938. The Parc des Princes is drenched in midsummer humidity, though a thin mist from the River Seine still clings to the flood-light halos. Newspapers have spent the week in raptures over Dietrich and Dalí, yet no art in the city will match the canvas of torn grass awaiting Brazil's centre-forward. Early in extra time against Poland—score knotted at 4-4—Leônidas da Silva pivots away from a puddle, pops the ball into the air with his instep, and hurls himself backward. For a second his boots eclipse the crossbar; for a second more his body forms a letter X against the glare. Then leather meets laces with a WHAP heard clear to the reporters' tribune. The ball rockets past goalkeeper Madejski, catches a bead of drizzle, and bulges the net like a startled eel.

Stunned silence breaks into a roar that the Parisian press will baptize LA CLAMEUR NOIRE—the black clamour—because the man who has just somersaulted into immortality is Afro-Brazilian and unapologetically luminous. In less than two weeks he will finish the World Cup as top scorer, earn nicknames ranging from "Diamante Negro" to "Homme-Gomme" ("Rubber Man"), and sell more French postcards than the Eiffel Tower. But in that instant, slapping mud off white shorts, Leônidas looks almost embarrassed, as if his body committed an indiscretion that etiquette hasn't caught up to yet.

He will insist later that the bicycle kick—CHUTE DE BICICLETA, CHILENA, call it what you wish—has no inventor, only evangelists. South American dockworkers had experimented with back-flipped clearances for years; Chileans claimed ownership, Peruvians counter-claimed. Yet Leônidas carried the move out of twilight myth and into the global spotlight. Before the hat-trick against Poland, European crowds had read about the acrobatic shot in liner-deck gossip; afterward, children from Montmartre to Manchester tried it on cobblestones, sending shoes flying into washing lines.

From Praça Onze to the World Stage

He was born in Rio's São Cristóvão district in 1913—less a boyhood than a proving ground of alleyway PELADA, barefoot sprints over crushed seashell. Skinny, asthmatic, he learned to arc his body like a sprung bow while leaping the trolley tracks that sliced through Praça Onze. At sixteen he entered the youth ranks of São Cristóvão FC, too wiry, according to scouts, to survive centre-half tackles. He compensated with elasticity: neighbours swore they once saw him evade a handbag-snatching dog by vaulting the animal mid-stride.

By 1932, wearing Bonsucesso's modest maroon, he attempted what Rio's papers curtly described as "a tumbling volley." Witnesses say the stadium fell silent, the ball struck the bar, but the audacity traveled faster than the result. Two weeks later the columnist Mário Filho introduced him to readers as O HOMEM ELÁSTICO, the elastic man, and the tag would mutate into "Rubber Man" when Paris-Match repeated it in 1938.

Brazil's national team, wrestling with the hangover of a 1934 World Cup fiasco, almost left him behind for France. Selectors distrusted his circusmania flair, and club owners fretted over insurance premiums for upside-down strikers. In training he disarmed them: sprint drills barefoot to toughen arches, sit-ups finished with a back-arch so extreme teammates pleaded with the physio to check his spine. At night he practised the bicycle kick with a medicine ball until his sacrum bruised purple; the heavier weight slowed the motion and taught him to locate the sweet spot with blind accuracy.

When the tournament began, France's sports dailies scrambled for metaphors. One analogised his mid-air pose to "LE VOL DU DAUPHIN" (the dolphin's flight); another to fairground trapeze. Defenders chose coarser language, especially after discovering he could change direction mid-flip by flexing hip adductors—physics textbooks had no diagram for that. In the quarter-final replay versus Czechoslovakia he struck again, prompting the Czech captain to petition the referee that "such contortions surely breach the spirit of the rules." The referee shrugged; FIFA had yet to imagine gravity as a disciplinary matter.

Barefoot in Bordeaux

Legend gilded itself in Bordeaux's swampy Stade Chapou. Minutes after kickoff, a Czech full-back raked his studs across Leônidas' boot, tearing the leather tongue clean off. Rather than leave the pitch, he removed both boots, tied the laces around his waist, and played on in socks that dissolved to cotton ribbons within minutes. Photographers captured the image of him, toes caked in clay, sprinting at half-shod opponents and scoring anyway. Brazilian radio commentators rhapsodized: "ELE CORRE DESCALÇO COMO MENINO DO MORRO!"—he runs barefoot like a favela kid. For European audiences still nursing colonial fantasies, the sight of a shoeless black athlete outclassing paid professionals packed the charge of prophecy.

Brazil fell in the semifinals to Italy's muscular catenaccio, but Leônidas returned for the third-place match and bagged two more goals against Sweden, sealing the BOTA DE OURO with seven in total. French reporters mobbed him at gala dinners, eager to inspect his "secret" spring-coil calves; couturiers begged him to endorse suspenders; a Montparnasse sculptor offered to cast his feet in bronze. He accepted none of it, saving his signature for a São Paulo chocolate manufacturer named Lacta.

The Chocolate that Outsold Coffee

Lacta's executives understood an inflection point when they tasted one. Brazil was urbanising, radio ownership surging, and consumer branding looking for heroes who transcended class pigments. Within weeks they re-launched their crunchy milk-chocolate bar under a new name—**Diamante Negro**—paying Leônidas a one-off fee that equalled five years' factory wages. The wrapper bore a stylised profile of the striker, head tilted skyward as if mid-bicycle, his surname in deco font gold. Slogans rolled out: "VIVER É BOM—COM DIAMANTE NEGRO É MELHOR" (Life is good—better with Black Diamond).

Cinemas screened adverts before newsreels; corner cafés displayed cardboard cut-outs of him juggling bonbons like footballs. Sales tripled in six months.

For the first time, a Brazilian athlete's body generated passive income outside gate receipts. The notion that physical genius could migrate into confectionery—and later boots, radio programmes, bank bonds—opened floodgates. Club presidents who had balked at colour bars now raced to sign black forwards; if Leônidas could sweeten chocolate profits, why not ticket stubs? Pelé's father, Dondinho, still semi-professional in Minas Gerais, clipped the ads and told his young son they signalled a new world.

Tactical Aftershocks

Coaches, too, recalibrated. European tacticians dissected film reels, freeze-framing the moment airborne hips aligned perpendicularly to the bar. In Bologna, Vittorio Pozzo lectured that "preventing the inverted volley begins two passes earlier," birthing the concept of delayed pressing. Hungarians called for zónavédekezés—zonal defence—arguing that the only sure antidote to acrobatics was cutting the supply line wide. In Argentina, River Plate's LA MÁQUINA rehearsed midfield rotations explicitly designed to create room for winger Carlos Peucelle to attempt his own chilena, thereby globalising the creative virus.

In Brazil, the shockwave went deeper than magnet boards. Street kids who once imitated Garrincha's shimmy now hung hammocks as makeshift crossbars, flinging themselves backward into sand until shoulders bruised numb. Coaches in São Paulo youth academies added gymnastic mats to training sheds. An epithet circulated: "QUEM NÃO VIRA, NÃO VIBRA"—if you can't flip, you don't feel the vibe.

The aerial artistry also catalysed discourse on race and modernity. White editorialists had long contended that black bodies brought exuberance but lacked "tactical discipline." Leônidas shredded that lie. His bicycle kick wasn't reflex; it was geometry—the calculation of ballistics, timing, and center-of-mass rotation. Journalists began describing black players as "intellectual" on the pitch, a semantic pivot whose after-ripple would reach sport science departments decades later.

War, Exile, and Late-Career Flourish

World War II smothered his ballooning European fame; international fixtures dwindled, and Brazil's government, wary of Axis spies, tightened exit visas. Flamengo leveraged the climate to coax Leônidas into a record transfer, parading him through Rio's streets atop an open car. Crowds pelted carnations; estimates say 50,000 jammed the Avenida Rio Branco, eclipsing presidential motorcades. Radio announcer Ary Barroso improvised a samba riff on the bicycle kick that carnival blocos replayed for years.

Not all chapters dazzled. Draft-board wrangles in 1941 landed him an eight-month jail sentence for forging military documents—proof that stardom offered no shield against bureaucracy. He resurged with São Paulo FC, leading them to five Paulistão titles and staging a photogenic chilena in 1948 that magazine **O Cruzeiro** splashed across a two-page spread. The sequence, shot at 1/500-second shutter, became anatomy text for would-be contortionists and adorned barbershops from Recife to Rosario.

Leônidas retired in 1950, two months before Uruguay's MARACANAZO gutted the nation. Reporters begged him to comment; he declined, concluding, "Idols must know when their applause is for the past." He opened a radio-repair shop, endorsed coffee beans, and quietly mentored local forwards on landing safely from aerial theatrics—more ankles are broken on descent than ascent, he cautioned.

When he died in 2004, Brazil paused afternoon programming for tributes. FIFA's online obituary called him the game's "first global trickster." Yet his deeper legacy lives in the slow-motion replay of any modern bicycle kick: the moment hips rise above shoulders, gravity holds its breath, and somewhere a child decides that audacity is the shortest distance between earth and glory.

At full stretch, chest to the sun, Leônidas taught football to dream in three-hundred-and-sixty degrees. Few remember the match score that Paris evening; everyone remembers the silhouette—boots slicing heaven in half. It is choreography written once on damp French grass and reenacted forever wherever a ball and an open sky conspire to make fools of pessimists.

Chapter 6   Ghosts in the Maracanã: The 1950 Final & National Trauma

On the morning of 16 July 1950, Rio de Janeiro woke to a hush that belied the size of the thing being born. Outside the half-finished concrete bowl of the Estádio Municipal—quickly christened MARACANÃ after the marsh birds that once nested on the site—vendors arranged thermos flasks beside mountains of pão de queijo, unsure whether the day's crowd would be a blessing or a siege. By noon the answer was visible from the air: human rivers flowed along Avenida Maracanã, men in white fedoras and women balancing parasols moving in tidal synchrony toward a single, untested colossus.

The figures are still contested—government tally, police log, bookmaker's estimate—but the safest midpoint hovers around 200,000 paid and unpaid souls crammed into a stadium approved for 155,000. Reporters joked that if you spilled your mate tea at row 62 it would splash a stranger's shoulder in row 38. People climbed exoskeleton beams, perched on radio relay boxes, crouched on the rim of the upper terrace like gargoyles. They had come to witness inevitability: Brazil needed only a draw in this final-pool match to claim their first World Cup. Their opponents, Uruguay, population two and a half million, entered the arena as fashionable supporting actors scheduled to bow politely at curtain call.

In government offices, champagne already chilled. Newspapers had run headline mock-ups—"BRASIL

CAMPEÃO DO MUNDO!"—ready for the press plates. The post office printed a commemorative stamp three days early. So certain was victory that the Federação Paulista band rehearsed HINO DO TRIUNFO instead of the national anthem; why waste bars on pessimism? In a private box, President Eurico Gaspar Dutra sat beside FIFA dignitaries, puffing a cigar rolled in Bahia leaf, his white uniform glowing beneath concrete vaults. The empire of optimism had no retreats.

The Whistle and the Whisper

Uruguayan captain Obdulio Varela, barrel-chested and unhurried, noticed the celebratory banners on his warm-up jog. He stopped, spat, and muttered, "Los de afuera son de palo"—outsiders are made of wood. In the tunnel, hearing Brazilian winger Zizinho hum the samba TOURADAS EM MADRID, Varela pivoted from defiance to theatre. He marched his men onto the pitch at walking pace, then insisted they parade a giant Uruguayan flag in slow, exaggerated homage to the host crowd. Every extra second shoved needle into local nerves, as if reminding them the match still required kicking.

Kick-off. A roar like tearing canvas. Brazil's white shirts fanned out in the WM formation; Uruguay's backline compacted into an iron semicircle. In the 17th minute, Ademir blasted a shot that skimmed the bar, and the stands erupted prematurely—some swear confetti drifted before anyone realized there was no goal. Uruguayan keeper Roque Máspoli punched the next corner over, then kissed the crossbar for luck; the gesture earned him two years of cartoon immortality in Montevideo tabloids.

Halftime struck at 0–0. Radios across the nation buzzed with forced cheer. Ary Barroso, Brazil's most famous commentator, broke protocol to plead on-air: "CALMA, MEUS AMIGOS, A DANÇA COMEÇA NA SEGUNDA METADE."—Relax, friends, the dance begins in the second half. Housewives in Bahia stirred feijoada with fingers crossed. In a Belo Horizonte bar, a miner etched "2×0" into the condensation on his glass, prophecy by moisture.

When the Earth Tilted

Two minutes after the restart prophecy seemed secure. Right-winger Friaca tore down the flank, beat full-back Matías González, and drilled a low shot that skidded under Máspoli's arm. The Maracanã convulsed. Firecrackers misfired into sleeves; strangers kissed until hat brims tilted. Somewhere in Recife, a seamstress loosed her week's wages into the air like confetti.

Back at midfield, Varela picked up the ball, argued with the English referee that Friaca was offside—he surely knew the claim was baseless—then held the debate for a full minute. "I wanted the noise to cool," he later confessed. Silence, he believed, breeds doubt.

In the 66th minute doubt found a boot. Varela threaded a pass to winger Alcides Ghiggia, who glided toward the by-line. Everyone expected the cross; keeper Moacir Barbosa stepped two paces off his post to parry what would never arrive. Ghiggia, seeing daylight, slapped the ball near-post. Net. The stadium gasped—a single, gutted inhalation—then exhaled nothing. Radio man Oduvaldo Cozzi stuttered "...Gol... de... Uruguai..." so softly technicians checked his microphone for failure. Barbosa stood rigid, arms hanging, as if the mistake were a physical weight pinning them earthward.

Eleven minutes left. The air turned viscous. Then, minute 79: another Uruguayan break, Pérez to Ghiggia, a scissors inside Bigode, shot low across Barbosa, far corner. Goal. A schoolteacher in row 28 fainted; a legionnaire on leave tore up his winning-bet slip before the final whistle. In the press box, writer Nelson Rodrigues described the silence as "O SILÊNCIO DE UM PLANETA INTEIRO DE LUTO"—the hush of a planet in mourning.

When English referee George Reader sounded full time, Uruguay's bench erupted, but their cheers sounded tinny in the vacuum. Confetti drifted like forlorn snow; brass instruments drooped mute; a national anthem unsung choked in piccolo valves.

Trauma in Real Time

What happens when 200,000 hearts snap at once? Diaries, radio tape, and bar-room yawps give fragments. A milkman named Silvio recorded in pocket notebook: "Crowd feels like a dead animal. We move but do not live." At the Bar do Gerson in Niterói, a patron was heard repeating, "It is a misprint, a misprint," long after the final scoreboard blinked 1–2. On Rua da Alfândega a sailor flung his transistor into a sewer grate; children retrieved it still hissing the foreign victory chant.

President Dutra disappeared from his box five minutes before the trophy ceremony, later claiming a security briefing. In truth, aides found him at a washbasin, dabbing forehead with linen, mumbling that a constitutional crisis might have been easier to manage than this.

Scapegoat Number 1

That night Barbosa could not leave the stadium; police feared riots. They escorted him through a tunnel of concrete catacombs to an unlisted taxi. In following months he would be refused hotel check-ins, denied managerial jobs, and once, legend says, turned away from gifting commentary tickets with the phrase: "The man who made Brazil cry cannot enter." In 1993, forty-three years later, he visited the Seleção's training camp; a federation official reportedly ordered him out lest his presence jinx the squad. Barbosa would remark near his death, "In Brazil the maximum prison sentence is thirty years, but my punishment has lasted a lifetime." ESPN.com

The Birth of Canarinho

The autopsy on the defeat dissected more than tactics. Within months, journalists blamed the all-white kit as colourless, unlucky, unpatriotic. In 1953 Rio paper CORREIO DA MANHÃ ran a public contest to redesign the uniform in flag colours—green, yellow, blue, white. The winning entry by Aldyr Garcia Schlee birthed the CANARINHO we know: yellow gold shirt, green trim, blue shorts. When Brazil next appeared at a World Cup, 1954 Switzerland, they wore sunlight on their chests, hoping colour might exorcise ghosts. Google Arts & CultureBBC

Echoes Across Generations

Rodrigues, the columnist, would revisit the trauma for decades, calling it "our Hiroshima with lace handkerchiefs." Sociologists traced a national neurosis of near-misses to that afternoon: the preference for carnivalesque flair over dour certainty, the dread of complacency. Economists even computed dips in stock-market activity for the fortnight after the loss.

For Uruguay, the match swelled national mythology. Ghiggia quipped, "Only three people silenced the Maracanã: the Pope, Frank Sinatra, and me," then added, "but I did it in colour." In Montevideo, schoolbooks gilded MARACANAZO alongside Artigas's revolution.

Brazil eventually healed, but scars show in ritual. No World Cup countdown passes without archived black-and-white footage of Barbosa's fatal lean. Television producers lower commentary volume three decibels when the clip airs, as if still tip-toeing around ghosts.

And the stadium itself? Renovated, reduced, techno-pulsed, yet at the 27-metre mark where Ghiggia struck, stewards swear compasses misbehave and television booms record a half-second echo. Some realities never fully recalibrate.

Coda in a Quiet Bar

One rainy evening in 2000, Barbosa, ageing and stooped, entered a modest bar in Praia Grande to watch Brazil play Bolivia in a qualifier. Younger patrons recognized him and fell uncomfortably silent. The barman, breaking tension, slid a beer across, house-paid. Barbosa raised the glass and said, "Let's hope tonight they mark the winger." Nervous laughter sparked, the room exhaled, and for one minute the ghost sat among them as a man again. Brazil won 5–0. Outside, the rain slackened; no statues fell, no curses lifted, yet the avenue lights flickered in something like forgiveness.

The Maracanazo remains the night Brazil learned beauty could betray and that football, for all its poetry, keeps a ledger as cold as history. Every chant of "É CAMPEÃO!" is sung a notch louder now, just to drown a lingering whisper from 1950 that asks, E SE? What if? The question drifts still, like confetti never swept, glinting under modern floodlights, waiting for anyone bold enough—or unlucky enough—to answer.

Chapter 7 Pelé at Seventeen: Sweden 1958 and the Invention of a Legend

Nobody packed for Sweden expecting magic. Snow flurries still jittered across Gothenburg's rooftops in late May, and the Brazilian delegation arrived with crates of woollen track-suits, industrial-strength coffee, and a medical dossier thicker than the team's play-book. Somewhere among the scalpels and clipboards stood a slim teenager from Três Corações, Minas Gerais, rubbing gloved hands together and trying to look older than his passport age: 17 years, 7 months, 1 day. Edson Arantes do Nascimento—Pelé by playground decree—would step onto Scandinavia's frost-nipped grass and tilt global football on a new axis.

A Laboratory in Hindås

Coach Vicente Feola had insisted Brazil train away from city temptations, so the squad decamped to Hindås, a lakeside village forty kilometres east of Gothenburg. There, kit-men strung washing lines between pine trees and discovered that cotton jerseys froze into cardboard at night; morning warm-ups began with players punching stiffness from their own sleeves. Doctor Hilton Gosling prowled corridors with vitamin tablets and thermometers, enforcing bedtimes and—rumour swore—having the hotel replace its female staff lest hormones sabotage recovery sessions. A dentist extracted more than three hundred diseased teeth in camp; a dietician doubled the rice ration to soothe suddenly ulcer-free stomachs. Everything about Brazil's 1958 expedition felt less like a sports tour and more like a controlled experiment in how to erase a national trauma.

The Psychologist's verdict

Chief among the white coats was psychiatrist João Carvalhaes, who subjected players to Rorschach blots and word-association drills, declaring Pelé "infantile, lacking the necessary fighting spirit," and Marking genius Garrincha "too abnormal to trust in high-pressure situations." Feola scanned the report, stuffed it in a drawer, and started both men in the crucial knockout rounds. Science could measure pulse rates; it could not yet quantify improvised joy.

From Injury Table to Quarter-final Hero

Pelé strained a knee in a warm-up friendly against Sweden's club IFK Norrköping and missed the opening two group fixtures. Teammates remember him in the stands, swaddled in blankets, weeping into the collar of his parka each time Brazil scored without him. Cleared for the third match, he danced through Soviet defenders for fun but failed to score—a tease of thunderstorms forming behind thin cloud.

They broke in full against Wales in the quarter-final. Minute 66: Didi threaded a pass into the box, Pelé cushioned it off his chest, swivelled, and stabbed a half-volley through goalkeeper Kelsey's legs. Youngest goalscorer in World Cup history, radio announcers screamed; back home, church bells in Bauru drowned passing trains.

Hat-trick in the Cold

Three days later, the Parc des Princes crowd watched him dismantle France with a 23-minute hat-trick: first a knee-trap and stabbed rebound, then an instinctive chest-and-volley, finally a feint around keeper Abbes before rolling the ball into an empty net. Reporters searched dictionaries for new adjectives; Garrincha joked the kid was "playing peteca with Europeans."

The Ballet of Solna

The final in Stockholm opened with Sweden scoring first, a chill dagger for Brazilian hopes. Then Vavá equalised. Five minutes into the second half, a looping cross found Pelé's back to goal. He cushioned ball to thigh, flicked it over defender Parling, pivoted through the snowfall of flashbulbs, and volleyed past Kalle Svensson before his boots touched ground. Later he added a header—Brazil 5, Sweden 2—and collapsed at full-time sobbing into captain Bellini's chest. In every future montage of genius, that thigh-flick-volley sequence would glint like a crown jewel.

Quiet Revolutions Behind the Curtain

Victory was not built on instinct alone. Team chef Nair Belo replaced butter with Brazil-imported manioc flour to replicate home cooking for sensitive stomachs. Gosling's training diary shows ice baths at 11 °C to quell muscle inflammation—commonplace today, radical then. Kit-man

Pedro Scapuzzi tested a lighter-weave sock to maximise sensation through the new green-trimmed boots. Even radio engineer Orlando Vasques rigged a pitch-side antenna so commentators in Rio received commentary without northern-latitude static, allowing 40 million listeners to live inside every Pelé feint.

The Birth of a Global Brand

Within hours of the final whistle, Swedish teenagers were practising back-garden bicycle kicks while chanting PEL-É, PEL-É—a name they'd mis-pronounced only yesterday. Santos FC's secretaries awoke to telegram offers for European tours at fees triple prior rates. In São Paulo, advertisers slapped the teenager's grin onto watch faces, tonic bottles, and a new tangerine soft drink called GINGA-COLA. One newspaper cartoon showed psychologists queuing for Pelé's autograph, diagnoses amended to "terminal genius."

Legacy in the Cold Air

Pelé flew home on a Varig Constellation, trophy seat-belted beside him. As the plane banked over Rio, clouds parted to reveal the Maracanã—still haunted by 1950—now shimmering gold in dawn light. A stewardess asked if he was afraid of expectations. He smiled: "I was born for goals, not ghosts."

Brazil's snow-kissed summer in Sweden re-engineered world sport: it legitimised sports psychology without letting it overrule intuition; it proved teenagers could own the grandest stage; it fused samba with Scandinavian air and witnessed destiny twirling on the boots of a boy who had once shined shoes outside Bauru station. Pelé did not just lift the Jules Rimet Trophy—he lifted Brazil's imagination past the reach of winter.

Chapter 8   Garrincha's Bent Path: 1962 and the Joy of the Dribble

The first thing most people noticed about Manoel Francisco dos Santos was the geometry—or, to European eyes, the mis-geometry—of his legs. His right limb bowed inward, his left curved outward, and one was six centimeters shorter than the other. Doctors in Pau Grande, the textile hamlet north of Rio where he was born in 1933, stamped him "physically disabled" and moved on. Street kids saw something else: a slingshot whose rubber never broke. When Garrincha dribbled, his hips drew parenthetical arcs, his knees signed their own calligraphy, and defenders felt they were tackling a question mark that kept changing punctuation.

Chile Without Pelé

Twenty-nine years later he landed in Santiago with the Brazilian squad and an injury list that made even optimists wince. Pelé had torn a thigh muscle in the second group match; Brazil's plan B seemed to involve prayers and liniment. Garrincha, who had never much cared for tactical diagrams, suddenly held the collective mood in his curved stride. Teammates remember him whistling samba licks on the team bus while journalists typed obituaries for Brazil's chances.

The quarter-final against England turned the obituary into epic. In the 31st minute Garrincha swerved around Ron Flowers, looked up, and thundered a left-foot drive that bent in off the post. Ten minutes later he outsprinted Bobby Moore down the touchline and crossed for Vavá. Final score 3-1, but it felt wider: Brazil had discovered that without Pelé's imperial gravity, Garrincha's mischief could run amok.

The Semi-final Carnival—and Scandal

Chile, hosts and sentimental darlings, packed Estadio Nacional for the semi. Garrincha responded by staging a private carnival: two goals (a header, then a 30-meter daisy-cutter), one assist, a sombrero flick that left full-back Rojas colliding with thin air, and a booking that would cast a shadow over the tournament. Late on, as tempers boiled, Chilean wing-half Landa kicked Garrincha's ankles; the Brazilian retaliated with a knee to the thigh. Referee Codesal flashed red.

Under FIFA statutes Garrincha was suspended for the final, but something unprecedented happened. Chile's own newspapers petitioned FIFA to pardon him; President Jorge Alessandri added a diplomatic nudge. They argued that the World Cup's showpiece deserved its jester. FIFA relented— quietly, to save face—and on 17 June Garrincha jogged into the Estadio Nacional with a low fever, paracetamol, and a nation's expectations. Brazil beat Czechoslovakia 3-1; the bent-legged winger, hobbling yet luminous, left the field clutching both the Jules Rimet trophy and the Golden Ball.

Off-Field Detours

Garrincha's legend is part choreography, part cautionary tale. He loved cachaça, fishing trips that lasted three days, and a samba singer named Elza Soares whom tabloids painted as a home-wrecker. Their affair began before the Chile World Cup; Elza followed him to Santiago incognito, fearing she would be blamed if Brazil lost. They married in 1966, endured poverty, violence, and paparazzi, yet her raspy anthem "Se Acaso Você Chegasse" still carries a whiff of Garrincha's swivel—unexpected, joyful, slightly tipsy.

Back in Rio he once crashed a borrowed Jeep into a lamp-post, injuring his mother-in-law and prompting magistrates to suspend his license for five years. Botafogo tried curfews; he slipped out windows. The national team hired chaperones; he shared their beer. Yet every lapse fed the folk-story: the angel with bent wings who could not fly straight off the pitch but soared on it.

Decline and Apotheosis

His knees, mistreated and un-rehabbed, gave out by 1969. Alcohol filled the vacuum. He died of cirrhosis in 1983, penniless, aged forty-nine. Forty-thousand mourners filed past his coffin in the Maracanã, chanting, "OBRIGADO, ALEGRIA DO POVO!"—thank you, Joy of the People. Newspapers wrote that Brazil buried more than a footballer; it buried the carefree part of itself that never quite returned after television, data analysts, and 4-4-2s tidied up the playground.

The Dribble That Outlived the Man

Tactically, Garrincha's 1962 exploits redrew defensive manuals. European coaches stationed a spare full-back ten meters behind the line—a primitive sweeper—to double-team any winger who dared mimic him. Physios began screening youth prospects for hip flexibility, wondering if genetics could predict genius. In Brazil, kids practising the DRIBLE DA VACA measured their success by whether the ball rolled on its own curve—"Garrincha spin," they called it.

Listen to stadium crowds when a modern winger pauses, drops a shoulder, and jinks inside: the collective inhalation is older than colour television. It is a memory of snowy Santiago afternoons, of a man whose legs disagreed on direction yet conspired to make defenders vanish. Pelé gave football its royal lineage; Garrincha gave it its grin.

Chapter 9   The 4-2-4 Blueprint: Tactics of Beautiful Chaos

The old Botafogo locker room still smelled of mothballs and liniment when Vicente Feola carried a school-teacher's blackboard through the door one muggy night in late 1957. He propped it on two Coca-Cola crates, dabbed the slate with dusty chalk, and drew four bold strokes across the back line, two short dashes in midfield, and four attacking arrows that almost pierced the frame. The players blinked. They had seen WM sketches, Swiss bolts, even the lopsided DIAGONAL systems of the 1940s, but never anything this nakedly audacious: **4-2-4**.

Feola tapped twice on the forward arrows. "These," he said, "are the chaos engines. Everyone else must furnish the calm."

Seeds from Budapest and Buenos Aires

The blueprint's genealogy reached well beyond that smoky locker room. In the 1930s a Hungarian named **Dori Kürschner** arrived at Flamengo with a pocketful of Central-European theories. He pushed full-backs wider, tucked a midfielder deeper, and coined the phrase JOGAR NA DIAGONAL—play on the diagonal. A decade later Brazilian coach **Flávio Costa** twisted Kürschner's ideas into an asymmetric WM that locals nicknamed simply A DIAGONAL. It encouraged wing-backs to surge and inside-forwards to glide into half-spaces long before the term existed.

Then came itinerant maestro **Béla Guttmann**, who breezed through São Paulo in 1953 hawking a more radical notion: subtract a defender, add a striker, and trust geometry to out-run anxiety. Brazilian assistants copied pages from his notebooks, translating arrows into Portuguese verbs— EMPURRAR (push), ROTACIONAR (rotate), SUSTENTAR (hold).

The Chalk Meets the Samba

Feola's genius was neither invention nor theft but **synthesis**. On training pitches at Santos and Botafogo he married European spacing to Brazilian improvisation, reminding full-backs Djalma Santos and Nilton Santos that their overlapping runs should finish with a BATUCADA of short passes, not speculative crosses. He drilled midfield pair **Zito** and **Didi** to operate like an accordion: one note deep, the other climbing, always compressing and expanding the sonic space between defense and attack. And he let the forward line—**Garrincha, Vavá, Pelé, Zagallo**—colour outside every pencilled edge.

The first full rehearsal took place behind closed gates at Vila Belmiro. A local journalist who bribed a groundsman for entry later wrote that play resembled "a marching band that suddenly learned to improvise jazz." When Pelé dropped twenty metres to collect the ball, Zagallo scissored inside to plug the vacancy; Garrincha stayed wide enough to ruffle corner-flag tassels; Vavá prowled the penalty arc like a shark sensing hemoglobin.

Sweden 1958: Proof of Concept

On Scandinavian grass the theory became folklore. Against the Soviet Union, Brazil's back four absorbed Lev Yashin's long goal kicks while Didi and Zito pin-wheeled possession until the front quartet found daylight. Garrincha smacked the post twice in two minutes; on the third surge Pelé's dummy froze a defender and Vavá slid in the opener. Commentators searching for European analogies settled on images of "two teams on the same pitch"—one coloured yellow, the other apparently invisible.

Coaches from Italy's CATENACCIO school huddled in the stands, sketching furious counter-measures: drop the sweeper deeper, anchor a second half-back ahead of him. None worked. Brazil sailed home with the Jules Rimet and a tactical export more intoxicating than coffee.

Chile 1962: Evolution under Duress

Four years later, with Pelé injured early, assistant-turned-selector **Aymoré Moreira** tweaked the blueprint rather than torch it. Zagallo slid back toward midfield, creating a compromise shape historians later coded 4-3-3. Yet the skeleton remained 4-2-4: full-backs marauded, dual pivots patrolled, two strikers hunted. Garrincha's four goals and innumerable elastic shimmies completed the study: beautiful chaos could survive the loss of its most gifted conductor.

Diagram on a Bar Napkin

On a damp Rio evening in 1963, Feola and Didi found themselves at the Amarelinho bar demonstrating their system to a sceptical sportswriter using beer-glass coasters as players. Didi nudged two coasters side-by-side. "We form the hinge," he said, flicking them forward and back with pianist's fingers. Feola stacked four more at the table's edge. "And these," he grinned, "are the drummers—never stop beating." By closing time the napkin looked like a Kandinsky: arrows, squiggles, coffee stains, tactical prophecy.

Ripples Across Continents

By the mid-1960s Benfica, Real Madrid, and even defensive-minded Argentina had sampled 4-2-4's wine. Defensive coaches insisted the formation was irresponsible; marketing departments called it "television football" because the wide spacing made for clearer broadcasts. In England, Alf Ramsey borrowed its forward press yet re-labelled his tweak the "Wingless Wonders," avoiding Brazilian flamboyance while pocketing its structure en route to 1966 glory.

Anatomy of the Chaos Engines

- **The Full-Backs:** Nilton Santos pioneered the under-lapping run, sometimes finishing moves thirty metres from his own zone. European scouts scribbled "left-back or left-winger? both."

- **The Double Pivot:** Didi's outside-of-the-boot passes stretched opponents horizontally while Zito's interceptions compressed them vertically. Opponents felt seasick: waves from two directions.

- **The Inside-Winger:** Zagallo invented the defensive winger, tracking opposition full-backs before knifing into the half-space. His stamina turned a foursome into a pendulum.

- **The Floating Ten:** Pelé blurred lines—striker, maker, decoy, destroyer—and by doing so forced man-markers to play zones they had never rehearsed.

Decline or Metamorphosis?

By 1970 Brazil's attacking riches persuaded coach Zagallo (now wearing the suit) to morph 4-2-4 into a carousel 4-3-3/4-5-1 hybrid. Analysts called it the death of the original formation; but if you freeze the tape the old bones still surface each time Jairzinho and Rivellino join Pelé across a high, four-man front. Further evolutions—Tele Santana's 1982 diamond, Scolari's 2002 box—echo the same principle: dual pivots stabilise so that at least four artists may paint with reckless colour.

Legacy on a Whiteboard

Every modern coach who deploys overlapping full-backs and a twin-screen midfield owes royalty to that chalkboard hauled into Botafogo's locker room. Jürgen Klopp's front quartet at Liverpool, Pep Guardiola's false-winger lanes, even the data-driven bursts of today's Seleção track lineages back to the 4-2-4's beautiful chaos. Structure married rhythm; calculation wed improvisation; and the world learned that geometry dances best when it hears a drum.

Chapter 10   Salt, Sand, and Street-Lamp Matches: How Environment Shapes Technique

The first ball of the morning drifts in from the South Atlantic. It is 5:42 a.m. on Copacabana, and the tide has receded just far enough to leave a band of hard-packed sand—nature's own training pitch—between the waterline and the kiosks. Two teenage girls wearing Flamengo singlets knock a battered Mikasa to each other while a hotel janitor rakes yesterday's cigarette butts into piles. Each touch sounds different: a dull THUNK when the ball meets damp sand, a sharper POP when the girls flick it back into the sweet spot of gravity. In thirty minutes the beach will belong to sun-seekers, but right now it is an outdoor biomechanics lab, testing ankles, knees, and hips at odd vectors.

The Sand Laboratory

Ask any carioca coach why beach football breeds velvet first touches and they will talk about ABSORÇÃO—absorption. Sand swallows momentum, forcing players to over-compensate with softer ankles and knees that bend deeper than they would on grass. The surface is a merciless tutor: heavy footing means the ball dies; too gentle and it skips away on a rogue grain. A 2024 FIFA beach-soccer manual notes that every volley demands "150 percent more concentric calf activation than on firm turf," turning each hop into a micro-plyometric drill.

Ronaldinho, who spent childhood holidays in Porto Alegre juggling shells, once told an interviewer that sand "teaches the ball to whisper." He might have been quoting physics. Trials at the Universidade Federal de Viçosa measured a 22-percent reduction in ball velocity after the first bounce on medium-grain beaches, buying an extra half-second of decision time—enough to invite a sombrero flick or no-look pass. That half-second, multiplied by thousands of seaside mornings, becomes muscle memory.

Asphalt Allegro

Shift inland two blocks, and the morning rhythm changes pitch. Under the elevated viaduct of Santa Teresa, road-builders have yet to arrive. Delivery cyclists chalk two stone piles nine meters apart and slide a half-deflated futsal ball onto cracked asphalt. In five-a-side PELADA, the ball never leaves the ground. Square centimeters, not yards, decide the duel. Every pass pings off uneven tar, forcing shin-angle micro-corrections that would give a sports-scientist vertigo.

A 2018 study in the JOURNAL OF EXPERTISE frames this bricolage as "environmental constraint-led learning" and credits Brazil's street textures with the development of "closed-chain proprioceptive calibration". In plain language: players learn to feel the bounce in their bones. A professional academy might preach repetition under controlled conditions; the favela does the opposite, feeding children an endless buffet of variables—gravel, potholes, soda-can obstacles—until adaptive control is reflex.

Night-Lamp Ballet: Futsal Courts after Dark

At 9 p.m. the same day, six kilometers north in the Tijuca district, halogen bulbs hiss to life over a concrete futsal court wedged between apartment blocks. Neon drift from a churrasquinho stand paints the far wall pink. The evening's line-up: three delivery-app riders fresh off shift, an orthodontist still in scrubs, a middle-schooler called Joãozinho whose mother watches from a window, and a grizzled taxi driver they affectionately nickname TIO.

Futsal, officially codified in Montevideo in 1934 but adopted with missionary zeal by Brazilian schools in the sixties, is the finishing school for the country's ball-wizards. The ball is smaller, heavier, and bounces thirty percent less than a regulation size-5, demanding ball-rolling plutôt que ball-chasing. Neuromotor studies on small-sided games find that 3-v-3 and 6-v-6 formats provoke up to 88 percent more individual technical actions per minute than 11-a-side scrimmages. More touches equal more learning trials; more trials equal deeper neural grooves.

Joãozinho fakes a shot, drags the ball with his sole, and rockets forward as if yanked by unseen cable. The taxi driver doesn't even bother turning—too slow on concrete. Sole-rolls, toe-pokers, and heel-flicks dominate because the futsal shoe's flat rubber outsole acts like a gecko pad, inviting low-centered improvisation. Years later the same kid might be wearing studs inside Camp Nou, but under these street-lamps he is writing the syntax of future highlight reels.

The Barefoot Advantage

One myth persists: that Brazilian children learn everything barefoot. While sponsorship money now delivers synthetic turf and Nike Mercurials to many academies, flat-foot textures remain formative. Recent research in FOOTWEAR SCIENCE shows barefoot multidirectional drills improve ankle-eversion control and plantar sensory feedback—which in turn correlate with rapid direction changes in football. In simpler terms, naked soles are better antennas.

Consider Marta Vieira da Silva, raised on the dirt lanes of Dois Riachos. She spent mornings dribbling orangish clay so abrasive it burned blisters through callus. "Shoes were for church," she laughs in interviews, crediting the tactile bond with earth for the half-beat hesitation dribble that became her trademark. When U.S. coaches tried to tweak her instep striking mechanics, they found she could not replicate the same ball-feel in padded boots. Solution: she slit the insoles thinner.

Copacabana Footvolley and the Vertical Touch

Afternoons on Copacabana evolve into footvolley tournaments. The net stands two meters high, demanding chest, shoulder, and head touches that volleyers call "third-floor play." Sand again dictates technique: jumping for a header costs more energy, so players learn to hop from a one-step gather, knees splaying outward to maintain balance on landing. Observational time-motion studies from the São

Paulo Sports Institute record an average of 312 touches per match— double the count in beach soccer—building aerial dexterity transferable to crossing duels and chest-control traps on grass.

Ronaldinho credits footvolley for the chest-knee-volley sequence he used to devastate Villarreal in 2006; Neymar used similar drills to perfect the mid-air sombrero he premiered against Juventus in 2017. The ball arcs differently in seaside humidity; mist adds micro-weight, rewarding players who master spin over pure power. Environment again scripts technique.

The Streetlight's Lens: Vision and Decision Speed

Urban play after dark provides another evolutionary quirk: compressed vision. Under sodium lamps, the periphery dims sooner, forcing rapid head checks and anticipatory scanning. A Frontiers 2021 article on socio-economic constraints argues that favela kids develop superior "radar" because poorly lit spaces sharpen dorsal-stream processing speeds.

Take a pickup game in Complexo do Alemão. The court is caged and the only illumination comes from a single municipal bulb. Players chalk their names in queue to challenge winners—winner-stays-on formats reward efficiency, not endurance. Vinícius Júnior, who grew up nearby, calls these matches "flash-futsal." He claims they trained him to read deflections before they occur, a trait Real

Madrid analysts later measured as shorter saccade-return intervals during La Liga matches.

The Role of Noise—Literal and Figurative

Technique is never formed in silence. Beaches pulsate with samba loops from portable speakers; streets echo motorcycle backfires; futsal courts reverberate with hip-hop and mothers scolding toddlers. Neural correlates of such "irrelevant" auditory stimuli include enhanced error-detection rates under variable practice—what sport scientists call the CONTEXTUAL INTERFERENCE EFFECT. A 2019 study in HUMAN MOVEMENT SCIENCE found that athletes training in noisy environments registered 14 percent faster correction times when confronted with unexpected ball deflections.

Practically, this means a Copacabana winger is already accustomed to filtering sensory static; a sudden whistle or crowd gasp in a 90,000-seat stadium is just another wave to surf.

Environmental Economics: Poverty as Innovation Accelerant

Not all stories are romantic. The same Frontiers paper dubs Brazil's grassroots system "the poor wealth of football." Scarcity forces bricolage: traffic cones for corner flags, milk crates as goals, fruit stands doubling as rebound walls. Yet scarcity is also a design-thinking incubator. When materials fail, creativity fills the gap. Researchers in the

"Contextualised Skill Acquisition" framework argue that such constraints compel players to solve movement puzzles, fostering what neuroscientists call DEGENERACY—multiple solutions for the same outcome.

Pelé once reminisced about learning to volley by kicking limes behind Bauru's train station. Limes split after three strikes; precision became non-negotiable. Contemporary academy players juggle size-5 balls in controlled drills; the lime juggler carries a curiosity that no curriculum can script.

Scientific Cross-Stitch: Variable Practice and Motor Learning

All these observations cohere under motor-learning theories. Variable-practice research suggests that constantly shifting task parameters—surface hardness, ball weight, lighting—enhances transferability of skills. Uehara et al.'s pelada study highlights how unstructured environments embed "repetition without repetition," the ecological equivalent of jazz variations. Small-sided futsal games double down on this principle, prescribing high-touch density and constrained space that accelerate technical bandwidth.

Even Brazil's elite academies now replicate favela chaos in micro-dose: Santos installs sand pits beside turf so U-13 players alternate surfaces; Flamengo schedules 5-v-2 rondos under strobe lights to simulate lighting fluctuations. Science chases folklore; tradition high-fives telemetry.

Case Study: Aterro do Flamengo Midnight League

Every Friday at 11 p.m., when Rio's Aterro do Flamengo park empties of joggers, an unofficial league kicks off under the glow of highway lamps. Entry fee: one six-pack for the after-party cooler. The pitch is part-pavement, part-patchy grass, lines drawn with sugar stolen from café sachets.

In 2009, a shy 14-year-old Philippe Coutinho snuck out of his aunt's apartment to play here against adults. The stories claim he learned his trademark outside-foot curl because a missing floodlight left one corner in darkness; bending the ball around shadows let him see where it landed. Whether apocryphal or not, the anecdote captures a truth: environmental quirks become technical signatures.

When Environment Travels Inside Stadiums

Modern arenas try to sterilize randomness—perfect turf, symmetrical lighting, climate-controlled roofs. Still, Brazil's schoolyard DNA leaks in. Watch Vinícius Júnior skip along touchlines, flicking the ball so it barely grazes grass as if to keep feet beach-dry; see Richarlison's no-look heel volley against Serbia—pure footvolley timing; admire Debinha's quick-sole drag in NWSL play, a futsal artifact. These are environmental stowaways smuggled into elite contexts.

Sports marketers package the aesthetic as **joga bonito**, but the phrase flattens complexity. Beautiful chaos is engineered, not accidental, by countless collisions between restless children and unforgiving surfaces.

Epilogue of a Day in Microcosm

The Copacabana sky dusks again. The two girls from dawn have showered, changed into school uniforms, and returned with textbooks underarm to watch tourist footvolley while nibbling coxinhas. The delivery cyclists from the asphalt game are already back on motorbikes, weaving traffic. Joãozinho's futsal court now hosts couples dancing forró under the same halogen lights. Technique seeps from one hour to the next, one surface to another, like ocean water wicking through sand.

If Brazilian football is a language, environment provides the accent. Sand rounds the vowels, asphalt sharpens consonants, futsal timings add syncopation, and night-lamp shadows supply the subtext. Each pitch is a classroom; each bounce is a question; every barefoot answer threads itself into the quilt of the JOGO BONITO.

Chapter 11 Mexico 1970: The Technicolor Symphony

Midday light in Mexico City behaves like nowhere else on Earth. High-altitude air thins the haze, bleaches colours sharper, and bounces sound off the bowl of the Sierra Madre until a murmur becomes a canyon echo. At 11:55 a.m. on 21 June 1970, that light rained through the open roof of the Estadio Azteca and struck two football teams standing at ease on the centre-circle rim. One wore a yellow so electric it seemed plugged into the sun; the other a blue that might have been cut from the Mediterranean. For the first time in World-Cup history most of the planet saw those hues live, in motion, via satellites perched 36,000 kilometres above. Mexico 1970 was colour television's coming-out party, and fate had booked Brazil to play the lead.

Beaming Brazil to the World

The broadcast infrastructure looked like the set of a science-fiction film: two INTELSAT III birds lashed signals to earth stations in Andover, Maine, and Goonhilly Downs, Cornwall; Televisa engineers in Mexico juggled time-code to feed both hemispheres. Around 600 million viewers—an audience larger than the combined populations of the competing nations—watched Pelé flex calf muscles under a noon sun hot enough to melt camera grease. Living-room sets from Lagos to Liverpool glowed with Canarinho yellow. For many viewers it was their first colour programme of any kind; decades later they could still describe the exact tint. The tournament's official ball cooperated: Adidas debuted the thirty-two-panel **Telstar**, black pentagons stitched between white hexagons for maximum contrast on monochrome televisions, a design now synonymous with "soccer ball" emoji.

Altitude, Heat, and the New Science

Altitude (2,200 metres) thinned lungs and floated long passes an extra metre. FIFA allowed water breaks—another first—and doctors carried portable pulse oximeters that chirped like crickets in the dressing rooms. Brazilian physio Mauro de Andrade dosed his players with beet-root capsules after a Swedish study suggested nitrate might widen blood vessels at elevation; nobody knew if it worked, but nobody cramped either. Players wore thin cotton jerseys soaked in ice water before kick-off; within ten minutes they were plastered to skin like tropical tattoos.

The Squad as Pop-Culture Ensemble

Coach Mário Zagallo, himself a two-time champion winger, arranged a moving mosaic: Clodoaldo the metronome, Gérson the compass, Rivellino the cannon-left foot, Tostão the false-nine before the term existed, Jairzinho the hurricane who would score in every single match, a feat still unmatched, and, orbiting above them, Pelé in imperial phase.

Jairzinho arrived with a private ambition: "If Pelé is the king, I'll be the thunder." He netted against Czechoslovakia, England, Romania, Peru, Uruguay, and Italy—in every colour that television could throw at him—earning the nickname

Furacão (Hurricane). European writers struggled to phoneticise his name; newspapers in Rome resorted to "Ya-EER-zeen-yo." It hardly mattered. Viewers had learned to recognise him by the piston thighs and the white sweatband he wore like a rebel's sash.

Pelé, Puma, and the Shoelace Heard 'Round the World

Minutes before Brazil's quarter-final with Peru, Pelé bent to retie a bootlace on the centre spot. All cameras zoomed in—how could they not?—catching a crisp close-up of the **Puma** logo. Rival brand Adidas, official tournament sponsor, fumed in the VIP box. What looked like an innocent pause was, in fact, a clandestine deal brokered by Puma executive Hans Henningsen: Pelé would halt play for a moment's shoelace adjustment, guaranteeing a global cameo worth an estimated US $120,000—small then, gargantuan now. The stunt is still cited in marketing courses as the day ambush advertising learned to dribble.

The Azteca Overture

Brazil waltzed through the group stage, survived Gordon Banks's impossible save and Bobby Moore's tackle in a 1-0 masterpiece against England, then swept past Peru (4-2) and Uruguay (3-1). Each match added musical layers: Rivellino's "Elástico" here, Clodoaldo's four-man shimmy there. Viewers gasped not merely at goals but at camera angles—slow-motion replays, reverse cuts—from which the ball seemed to glide on rails of pure geometry.

4-1 Against Italy: The Goal That Became Scripture

Minute 86, final already 3-1, Italy pushing up in desperation. Tostão traps a clearance near Brazil's left corner flag and toes it to Clodoaldo. The midfielder swivels, pirouettes past **four** Azzurri in ten metres—first vignette in the montage. He releases to Rivellino, who slides a diagonal to Jairzinho hugging the paint of the right touch-line. Jairzinho slows—one breath, two—drawing defender Rosato, then bursts inside. As he nears the box he spots Pelé, statuesque in the D, and squares the ball.

Pelé, who has already scored with a header and assisted Jairzinho, takes a single, unhurried touch. It is the photographic negative of speed, a silence in orchestral swell. Out of frame, right-back **Carlos Alberto** is sprinting into the shot with the commitment of a dive-bomber. Pelé looks left, looks right, judges the bounce, then rolls the ball sideways at the precise weight where Alberto will not need to break stride.

The captain arrives, draws back his right leg, and lashes a cross-goal drive so true it burrows into netting before Italian keeper Enrico Albertosi can collapse. Nine passes, twenty-one seconds, half the team involved, culminating in a full-back finishing from open play. Aesthetes would later call it football's Sistine Chapel; YouTube libraries have it bookmarked under "Greatest Goal Ever."

Choreography Under the Microscope

Break the goal frame by frame and patterns emerge:

1. **Spatial Compression and Expansion** – Clodoaldo's dribble drags Italy's midfield blanket left; Rivellino's long diagonal snaps it right like a sudden cymbal crash.

2. **Third-Man Run** – Jairzinho's pause is bait; Carlos Alberto's overlap is the unseen dagger.

3. **Temporal Dissonance** – Pelé's leisurely pass amid ninety-minute fatigue is a magician's misdirection; viewers feel the lull before the lightning.

Modern analysts measuring "packing rate" (how many opponents are bypassed by each pass) score the move at seven—elite even by today's metrics. Yet stats miss its mood: an orchestra hitting crescendo, players instruments tuned to the same emotional key.

Commercial Crescendo

Within hours, corporate switchboards rang like church bells. Italian TV rights-holders, fearing riots, replayed only Italy's equaliser in post-match news. Everywhere else the world looped Carlos Alberto's thunder-bolt. Telefunken sold out of colour sets in Buenos Aires despite Argentina's absence from the finals. Panini's Mexico 70 sticker album went through six reprints. Brazilian embassies received requests for yellow jersey replicas; rumours claim some posted samples in diplomatic pouches.

The simple black-and-white Telstar became a global motif; children who had never kicked a ball drew thirty-two panels on classroom notebooks. Adidas sales vaulted 40 percent in the United States, a market previously indifferent to soccer. When FIFA calculated sponsorship fees for West Germany 1974, numbers had quadrupled; Mexico 70 had taught them the worth of colour television, star charisma, and a ball that looked good spinning across 525-line cathode rays.

Cultural Echo

In music clubs from Lagos to London, funk and soul bands renamed themselves "Canarinhos." Andy Warhol silk-screened Pelé's portrait on fluorescent canvas. Japanese manga artist Yoichi Takahashi, then ten years old, sketched the Carlos Alberto goal in margins of his mathematics workbook; a decade later he would create "Captain Tsubasa," inspiring countless J-League careers. The aesthetic of bright kits, long hair, and no-look passes seeped into pop culture like dye in fabric.

Tactical Legacy

Italy's coach Ferruccio Valcareggi defended the 4-1 scoreline by calling Brazil "unplayable in colour and heat." European clubs took a different lesson: space-hunting full-backs and forward-breaking midfielders could stretch any

The world had watched in colour and decided it preferred its football painted bright. The JOGO BONITO was no longer just Brazil's national dance; it was a broadcast signal, looping endlessly through space, calling everyone to the next carnival.

Chapter 12 Telê Santana's Dreamers: The Artful 1982 Squad

The elevator at the Hotel Presidente in Barcelona opened onto a scene that looked more like a philosophy symposium than a pre-World-Cup team talk. Zico was diagramming angles with an espresso spoon, Falcão twirling a wine cork to show rotational passing lanes, and Sócrates—shirt unbuttoned to the sternum—leaned back in an armchair quoting Rousseau on freedom. Telê Santana, the man who had gathered this constellation, watched from the doorway and grinned. "If the ball ever gets bored," he said, "she can always join the conversation."

Santana's 1982 Brazil were not merely a football team; they were an argument in motion. At a moment when the military regime that had ruled Brazil since 1964 was in its stumbling last act, Santana proposed a tactical manifesto as radical as any street-corner pamphlet: play joyfully, push full-backs high, let midfielders improvise triangles until opponents lose the plot. "Winning is important," he told reporters, "but beauty is independence." The country—aching for both—fell hard for the idea.

A Backdrop of Dissidence

Outside the training camp, São Paulo's Corinthians club was fomenting **Democracia Corinthiana**, a player-run experiment in workplace democracy led by Sócrates himself. Team selections, wage structures, even mealtime menus were voted on by raised hands—a direct affront to authoritarian Brazil. Sócrates vowed to move to Italy if Congress failed to restore free elections; banners at domestic matches carried the slogan "GANHAR OU PERDER, MAS SEMPRE COM DEMOCRACIA."

Santana did not replicate that voting model with the Seleção, but he shared its ethos. Staff meetings lasted until dawn because tactics doubled as ethics: How many forwards can you field before hubris becomes tyranny? Does a defensive midfielder restrict freedom or protect it? Full-back Júnior quipped that Santana "coached with a guitar pick"—always looking for the next chord rather than banging the same drum.

Anatomy of a Daydream Side

Santana sketched a 4-2-2-2 that blurred into a 2-4-4 during possession. Júnior and Leandro marauded so high they nearly shared a postcode with strikers Sérginho and Eder. Behind them:

- **Falcão** – the metronome from AS Roma, stride like a tango step, eyes that scanned two moves ahead.

- **Cerezo** – the fixer, sliding between lines to cover for fireworks elsewhere.

- **Zico** – the conductor with a flamethrower right foot.

- **Sócrates** – the philosopher-forward, a two-touch savant whose back-heel could launch counter-arguments as easily as counter-attacks.

Goalkeeper Waldir Peres, often lonely, called matches "viewings of Baroque paintings—sometimes you forget there's a frame."

Spain '82: Carnival on Grass

The group stage was a samba rehearsal: 2-1 over the USSR after Zico's scissor kick, 4-1 over Scotland drenched in Spanish sun, 4-0 over New Zealand with Sócrates drinking water only at half-time because he preferred beer after matches. Commentators swooned; British newspapers printed Zico's goal coordinates like art-gallery catalogues.

At night the team commandeered hotel pianos. Santana tolerated the ruckus, believing music tuned spatial awareness. Physio Manoel Leme complained only once—at 3 a.m., when a conga line threatened to sprain half the squad.

Sarriá, 5 July 1982: Beauty Meets Its Nemesis

Brazil needed only a draw against Italy in the second-round mini-group. Rumour has it Santana never considered parking a bus—he didn't even own the keys. Six minutes in, Paolo Rossi exploited a loose back-pass: Italy 1, Brazil 0. Sócrates equalised after a one-two with Zico that parted blue shirts like theatre curtains. Rather than settle, Santana signalled for more pressing. "Draws," he liked to say, "are conversations that trail off."

Rossi again, just before half-time. Falcão equalised with a left-foot laser that made the Sarriá's wooden terrace quake; he roared at Santana—"Agora, chefe?" Now can we lock the door? Santana circled a finger forward. Minute 74: corner kick, Rossi hat-trick. Brazil 2, Italy 3. World-Cup exit. Zico fell to his knees; Sócrates stared at a scoreboard that seemed to mock arithmetic. Falcão refused to leave the pitch until stewards nudged him. Years later he told THE GUARDIAN, "Rossi had three touches and scored a hat-trick. Football as we knew it died that day."

Post-Mortem in the Press

Brazilian headlines mourned a "tragedy of naïveté." Pundits attacked Santana for fielding attacking left-back Júnior against Italy's counter. A São Paulo columnist compared the team to a bossa-nova trio playing lullabies while thieves emptied the apartment. Yet abroad, writers hailed them as the best side never to win: LA GAZZETTA dubbed Brazil "i vincitori morali"—moral victors; Spanish fans chanted "Brasil, Brasil" as they left the Sarriá. Defeat looked, paradoxically, like conquest.

Why Artistry Lost

Historians have suggested four culprits:

1. **Goalkeeping Gap** – Peres was an able shot-stopper but not a sweeper; Rossi poached in that vacuum.

2. **Recovery Speed** – The high line asked 30-year-old centre-backs Oscar and Luizinho to sprint like wingers; physics declined.

3. **Altitude Hangover** – Matches at sea-level lacked the aerobic sting Brazil had weaponised in Mexico 1970; yet Santana did not rotate.

4. **Philosophical Stubbornness** – Santana's refusal to chase a draw mirrored Sócrates's refusal to compromise with generals; glory or bust.

Coaching manuals cite the game as a case study in risk management; romantics cite it as proof that risk is the point.

The Beauty That Endured

Within months Santana was rehired—public outcry demanded it. He prepped a 1986 sequel featuring Careca and Müller but injuries hobbled the cast. Santana never lifted a World Cup, yet a poll of Brazilian fans in 2018 ranked the '82 team second only to 1970 in affection. ESPN hailed them as "specialists in losing now serving as inspiration."

Pep Guardiola keeps a DVD of Brazil–Italy on his office shelf; he once told GOAL that watching Falcão orchestrate the midfield "showed me football could be music." Deportivo La Coruña renamed a training pitch "Campo Telê Santana." Nike's late-1990s JOGA BONITO ads lifted choreography straight from Zico highlight reels. Losing, it turned out, could be a louder megaphone than winning.

Sócrates died in 2011; at his funeral fans chanted "SE PERDER, VOU GANHAR!"—If I lose, I still win. Falcão became a senator, Zico coached in Japan and India, Júnior a TV pundit who ends broadcasts by humming the anthem from 1982. Santana, who passed in 2006, left behind a single quote carved on a plaque at São Paulo FC's academy: **"O futebol é arte quando a bola sorri."** Football is art when the ball smiles.

It never smiled wider than in the summer of 1982—when philosophers wore armbands, midsoles sang sambas, and a coach gambled immortality against pragmatism and, by losing, won.

Chapter 13   From Samba to Set Pieces: Adapting to Europe's Game

When Careca landed at Capodichino Airport in July 1987 he stepped into a swirl of horn blasts, police whistles, and Neapolitan dialect so quick it felt sung more than spoken. Banners read **BEM-VINDO CARICA**—close enough—and motorcycle escorts parted crowds like fish around a prow. Two hours later, in a rented apartment overlooking the Gulf of Naples, the striker from Campinas opened his diary: "FIRST SHOCK—MARADONA DOES NOT WARM UP, HE REHEARSES FREE-KICKS AS IF CARVING MARBLE." Shock number two arrived the next morning, courtesy of coach Ottavio Bianchi: forty-five minutes of **shadow runs** with no ball. "Italy trains absence," Careca wrote, "so the ball becomes a luxury you must earn."

That sentence could serve as thesis for an entire epoch. Between 1986 and 1994 more than a hundred Brazilian footballers crossed the Atlantic, lured by hard currency, live TV rights, and the glamour of a Serie A calling itself "il campionato più bello del mondo." Spain followed, then Portugal, Germany, and Holland. Airports began to look like talent auctions. For the first time since Charles Miller's suitcase, the flow of ideas ran strongly east-to-west—and it would rebound, forever altering the Seleção's compass.

Why the Exodus?

Brazil's economy in the late 1980s resembled a malfunctioning metronome: hyper-inflation topped 1 500 percent, clubs paid wages in crumpled instalments, player unions threatened strikes that never fully materialised. European presidents saw opportunity. Napoli wired $8 million for Careca; Roma had already spent $6 million for Falcão; PSV Eindhoven snagged a teenage Romário for what director Harry van Raaij called "peanuts sprinkled with samba." A PLACAR magazine cover blared **"Ouro de Gênova: dinheiro que fala italiano"**—Genoa gold: money speaks Italian.

Catenaccio 101: Life inside the Italian Laboratory

Serie A in 1987 was a cathedral to shape and cynicism. Training sessions at Napoli began with thirty-minutes **tattica a secco**—tactics without ball—players sliding on rails of chalk like pieces on a war board. Neapolitan journalist Mimmo Carratelli remembers Careca pleading, "One touch, Mister?" and Bianchi replying, "Touch the space, not the ball."

Alemao, the curly-haired volante from Rio, kept meticulous notes in a notebook eventually published by a Brazilian sports university. Sample entry: "CORNERS HERE ARE ALGEBRA: EIGHT REHEARSALS, THEN A NINTH WHERE COACH REMOVES A CONE TO TEST IF WE STILL SEE THE LINE." He learned that zonal marking meant trusting neighbours more than reflex; he learned to study opponents' hips instead of the ball. Years later, Alemao would drill the same habits into a young Cafu at São Paulo FC, proof that knowledge repatriates like migratory birds.

Spanish Pressing and the Gospel according to Cruyff

While Italians worshipped geometry without risk, Johan Cruyff's Barcelona—launched in 1988—preached space as invitation. Brazil's envoy to this academia was Romário de Souza Faria, who arrived barefoot on the steps of Camp Nou for his medical, sandals tucked in waistband. Cruyff's first demand: drop ten pounds; second demand: learn to press on triggers. Romário bristled ("I hunt, not herd"), yet within months video analysts showed him how a three-metre sprint at the right angle could buy eight metres of transition for Hristo Stoichkov. Romário adapted just enough, scoring 30 league goals and ushering Barça to a 1994 title—evidence that pressing could duet with samba if choreographed correctly.

Deportivo La Coruña ran a parallel experiment with Bebeto and Mauro Silva: one, a wispy finisher; the other, a midfield safety brake. Spanish fitness coach José Luis Seabra recalls Mauro repeating **"ver, pensar, correr"**—see, think, run— like a catechism. He logged teammate tendencies, marking arrows on notepaper: "DONATO LATE TO PIVOT ON THROW-INS; COVER GAP." That notebook, smuggled back to Brazil in 1993, became reference for manager Carlos Alberto Parreira as he plotted the Seleção's shape for USA '94.

Culture-Shock Vignettes

1. **Food:** Falcão at Roma hired a private cook to recreate FEIJÃO TROPEIRO but discovered olive oil lightened his joints; he never went back.

2. **Weather:** Dunga's first winter with Fiorentina saw him training in sleet; he mailed thermal tights to his brother in Rio with the note, "TELL THE KIDS THE WORLD IS COLDER THAN WE DREAM."

3. **Language:** Jorginho at Bayer Leverkusen stuck colour stickers on locker-room objects (rot, blau, gelb) until teammates nicknamed him PROFESSOR.

4. **Racism:** Aldair recalls monkey chants in Verona; he responded by standing still and applauding the curva, a gesture later studied in sociology classes as "RESIGNIFIED DEFIANCE."

Set-Piece Apprentices

Perhaps the most conspicuous export from Europe to Brazil was the cult of the dead ball. Italian sessions dedicated an hour solely to defensive corner routines, players numbered 1-11 on bibs to simulate real assignments. Leonardo, then at Valencia, compiled VHS tapes titled "Foul Variations—Near Side" and played them during national-team camps. By 1994 Brazil's marking at corners had tightened; by 2002, under Luiz Felipe Scolari, set pieces delivered nearly 40 percent of tourney goals—numbers unthinkable in the free-samba '70s.

Hybrid Returns: USA '94 and the Era of MODERNINHO

Parreira's triumph in Pasadena relied on Europeanised DNA: Dunga's midfield mulch, Mauro Silva's positional lid, Jorginho and Branco as disciplined full-backs. Italy's Arrigo Sacchi sniffed that Brazil had "sold its soul for a clean sheet," yet the trophy parade down Avenida Paulista convinced a generation of presidents: hybrid wins.

Youth academies shifted: Grêmio installed video rooms; Vasco da Gama hired an Italian fitness coach to teach "Periodizzazione." Even futsal drills began to include defensive rotations—kids shouting "BASCULAÇÃO!" on asphalt previously reserved for flamboyant nutmegs.

The Counter-Reformation: Artistry Strikes Back

Purists mourned. Zico argued on TV Globo that over-systematising risked sterilising GINGA. Rivaldo, returning from Deportivo in 1997, told reporters European coaches "tie shoes to ankles"; he loosened laces before each Brazil game "to feel wind between the toes." The debate sharpened after France '98 when a tactically mature yet Neymar-less Brazil froze in the final. Could a team both calculate and enchant?

Case Study: The Cafu-Roberto Carlos Corridor

Italian discipline met Brazilian audacity in the personalities of Cafu (Roma) and Roberto Carlos (Inter then Real Madrid). Both absorbed European defensive metronomes yet remained high-octane attackers. In 2002 they formed the fastest supply line in World Cup history—averaging 80-metre overlaps every three minutes—while still executing zonal recovery patterns honed at Milanello and Valdebebas. Analysts coined the term **"lateral turbo-marcador."** Kids in Recife practised shuttles shouting "ITALIANO PRA TRÁS, BRASILEIRO PRA FRENTE."—Italian backward, Brazilian forward.

Tactical Feedback Loops

By the mid-2000s idea exchange became frictionless: Brazilian analysts at Chelsea emailed heat maps to CBF headquarters; São Paulo's medical staff sent isokinetic data to AC Milan's Lab. The Seleção's 2006 flop, ironically, came from information overload—too many chefs, not enough seasoning. But the long arc bent toward syncretism: European clubs adopted Brazilian rondos; Brazilian clubs installed European GPS vests.

Diaries as Anthropology

The Brazilian Football Museum in São Paulo now displays a glass case of player notebooks:

- **Careca's 1988 entry:** "LEARNED TO MARK SPACE BETWEEN POSTS AT CORNERS—NO CHASING SHADOWS."

- **Dunga, March 1990:** "CATENACCIO IS THE ART OF WAITING WITHOUT SLEEPING."

- **Bebeto, April 1993:** "PRESS FIRST PASS, NOT SECOND; SPANISH RULE."

- **Rai, Dec 1994, Paris:** "IN FRANCE THEY MEASURE SLEEP; COACH SAYS REM EQUALS RECOVERY AS MUCH AS LAPS. SCIENCE IS SAMBA IN SLOW-MOTION."

Schoolchildren reading the diaries today trace arrows with fingertips as if decoding treasure maps—paths their heroes walked so that GINGA could glide on new floors.

The Modern Seleção: A Pendulum Settled?

Fast forward to 2019: Tite's Brazil wins Copa América with a back-four block straight from Serie A notebooks and a front trio doing TikTok choreography. Players arrive fluent in three lexicons: futsal angles, Italian compactness, Spanish counter-press. The pendulum no longer swings wildly; it hums, equilibrium found somewhere between a samba drum and a metronome click.

Coda: A Training Pitch at Cotia

Sunset splinters through eucalyptus at São Paulo FC's youth complex. Two U-15 squads scrimmage 7-v-7. Coach divides five minutes: first minute barefoot on sand rectangles, second minute on grass triangles, third on small-box rondo with mandatory two-touch, fourth on set-piece rehearsal with cones labelled in Italian (PRIMO PALO / SECONDO PALO), fifth on free play, "Show me your street trick." Boys giggle while executing scissors into zonal snaps. The hybrid is now default; the ball belongs to everyone and no one.

Brazil left home in the late 1980s chasing hard currency and found, in Europe's rigid corridors, mirrors that sharpened its own silhouette. What returned was neither samba nor set piece but a duet—discipline nodding to flair, flair winking back. And the dance goes on, a passport stamped in chalk lines from Napoli to Barcelona and back to Ipanema, proof that football's richest choreography is written on the move.

Chapter 14   Joga Bonito™, Inc.: Advertising, Sneakers, and Soft Power

The first swoosh on a Brazil shirt announced itself quietly: a thumbnail-sized logo stitched beneath the CBF crest during a 1996 friendly in Recife. No broadcast commentator mentioned it, but merchandising managers at Nike's Beaverton headquarters erupted in high-fives. Months earlier the company had closed a ten-year, $160-million contract with Brazil's federation—an audacious wager that the planet's most watchable team could become the planet's most lucrative brand. In the decades that followed, Brazilian flair would be packaged in 30-second epics, airport terminals would become dance floors, and a Portuguese phrase—JOGA BONITO, "play beautifully"—would morph into a trademarked sales engine.

The Swagger Ad

Nike's football courtship began at the 1994 World Cup with a brooding gladiator spot titled **Good vs Evil**, but the company's house style truly married Brazilian rhythm in 1998. Director John Woo was scouting locations for a Hong Kong action film when Wieden + Kennedy creatives phoned: "Can you shoot a heist movie in Rio's airport—only the thieves are footballers?" Three weeks later Paris-bound passengers watched as Ronaldo, Romário, Denílson, and Roberto Carlos dribbled luggage carousels, nut-megged security guards, and slid on polished tile until the final shot of the ball thudding against the departure-gate post. The commercial aired in eighty countries and taught advertisers a lasting truth: nobody sells happiness like a Brazilian with time and a football.

Behind the scenes, flight information boards were re-programmed to spell GOOOOL; Roberto Carlos filmed his tunnel slide thirteen times to beat friction burn. Nike's global market share in football boots jumped five percent that quarter, and airport security chiefs worldwide reported spikes in travelers attempting step-overs with carry-on bags. A Paris customs officer quipped, "We've seized more imaginary footballs than contraband."

The $50-Boot and the Hierarchy of Dreams

Until the mid-1990s, Brazilian children learned the game barefoot or in plastic CHUTEIRA MEIA ("sock shoes") sold at street markets for a few reais. Nike's entrance recalibrated aspiration. In São Paulo's Grajaú district, shop-fronts began advertising the **Nike Mercurial**—chrome-striped, 200 grams, elastomer studs—at roughly half a month's minimum wage. Kids pressed faces to glass, tracing boot contours in foggy breath. Mothers negotiated layaway plans: twelve instalments for a synthetic promise of acceleration.

Sociologists at the University of Brasília later called this consumer switch "boot fetishism"—equipment eclipsing equipment-less genius. Yet the swoosh also funded grassroots pitches: as part of its CBF deal, Nike bankrolled 300 mini-courts in low-income boroughs, each opening choreographed with a freestyle show and a pop-up kiosk of affordable replica shirts. The contradictions were baked in:

philanthropy on one sideline, product pipelines on the other.

The $100 Million Cage

In spring 2002 Nike unveiled **Secret Tournament (Scorpion KO)**—twenty-four superstar players locked in a shipboard cage, first-goal-wins, Elvis remix pumping like carnival drums. Directed by Terry Gilliam, the three-part series cost an estimated $100 million and arrived with pop-up cages in 13 capital cities where teenagers reenacted the ads for prizes ranging from T-shirts to scouting trials. A Time magazine columnist called it "the halftime show capitalism was born to stage."

Brazil, of course, won the real-life World Cup weeks later, and sales of the oval-neck yellow shirt spiked so hard that counterfeit factories in Paraguay were forced onto double shifts. Customs seized entire truckloads at the Foz do Iguaçu border; the black market simply raised prices. Swagger had become a currency; the swoosh its mint.

Virality Before the Word Existed

Three years later Ronaldinho, newly anointed FIFA World Player of the Year, filmed a boot-launch video in Barcelona's training dome: open briefcase, lace gold Tiempo Legends, juggle ball, volley off crossbar four times without letting it drop. Whether the feat was digitally stitched or divine physics mattered less than the upload date—October 2005. Within weeks the clip became the first YouTube video to cross one million views, nine months before Google bought the platform. Online virality had found its dribble, and marketing executives worldwide scribbled: "Make consumers ASK if it's real."

Joga Bonito—The Sermon

With the 2006 World Cup looming, Nike turned from spectacle to morality play. Eric Cantona, dressed in preacher-black, fronted a series called **Joga Bonito** that chastised diving, time-wasting, and negative tactics. Ads cut between carefree Brazilian futsal scenes and footage of cynical fouls, urging "play beautifully." Some coaches scoffed—Brazil themselves exited the Cup in pragmatic disarray—but the slogan tattooed itself onto language. FIFA Fair Play committees quoted it in press releases; amateur tournaments from Lagos to Los Angeles adopted it as code of conduct. A trademark had become an ethic.

Soft-Power Dividend

Brazil's Ministry of Foreign Affairs noted that tourist visa requests rose 18 percent between 1998 and 2007, citing "football culture" as the prime lure. During Lula's first presidential term, Nike co-sponsored trade fairs in Johannesburg and Shanghai where factory demos showcased both footwear tech and Brazilian steel. Economists coined the phrase "swoosh diplomacy" for the halo effect: every Carlos Alberto Torres autograph session inside a Nike Pavilion came with pamphlets on Amazonian eco-travel and Petrobras investment windows. If Pelé once sold Brazil's soul as carnival, Nike sold its body as lifestyle portfolio.

The Price of Famished Hope

Yet commercialization carried collateral. In Maranhão, a youth coach complained that ten-year-olds refused to train in generic boots. In Rio, amateur leagues introduced footwear checks to curb stud injuries from cheap knock-offs. Journalists wondered if street ingenuity was being squeezed by the funnel of brand scripting—if the ball's old rebellious grin now flashed a corporate smile.

Still, ask Thiago Silva about his childhood in a Jacarepaguá housing block and he'll recall copying airport-ad moves under sodium lamps. Ask Marta and she'll cite Ronaldinho's gold-boot clip as proof a farm girl could mesmerize the world without a TV contract. Branding, for better and worse, expanded the map of possible futures.

The Swoosh in Retrospect

A quarter-century after Nike's quiet arrival, Brazilian football toggles seamlessly between favela court and influencer set. Vinícius Júnior TikToks footwork in limited-edition Phantom GXs; teenage freestylers livestream cage tricks sponsored by telecom giants; CBF academies track prospects via GPS vests whose data feed straight to Oregon. The swoosh may never replace the samba beat, but it has leased permanent space inside its rhythms—proof that in the global bazaar of dreams, style always finds a buyer, and the buyer always sells another dream.

Chapter 15   R-R-R: Romário, Ronaldo & Rivaldo Rewrite the '90s

The decade opened with a swaggering boast scrawled on a Rio changing-room whiteboard: "SÓ PRECISO DE UMA BOLA E 90 MINUTOS." I need only one ball and ninety minutes. The handwriting belonged to **Romário de Souza Faria**, five-foot-six of razor-edged self-belief who would spend the 1990s proving—then re-proving—that football's most valuable real estate is the twelve yards between penalty spot and goal-line. By the time the millennium closed, two more Rs had joined him on Brazil's marquee: **Ronaldo Luís Nazário de Lima**, the hurtling comet with thighs like hydraulic rams, and **Rivaldo Vítor Borba Ferreira**, the lank-limbed left-footer who bent physics to melancholy poetry. Between them they delivered one World Cup (1994), lost another in Shakespearean fog (1998), and reclaimed the crown in 2002, leaving behind a triptych of ego clashes, back-heel assists, hospital monitors, fines, and redemption arcs no screenwriter would dare compress.

Act I   Romário and the Soloist's Rhapsody (USA 1994)

Brazil arrived in the United States under a cloud of doubt thick enough to blot out a California sun. Telê Santana's dreamers had fallen in 1982 and 1986; Carlos Alberto Parreira, the new pragmatic coach, heard pundits sneer that he was appointing accountants to conduct a samba school. His solution was a 4-4-2 lattice whose diamond tip glinted whenever Romário dropped his shoulder.

From the opening game against Russia in the Silverdome, Romário moved like a cat burglar in fluorescent boots—minimal steps, maximal incision. Against Cameroon he scored after a 40-yard Bebeto pass that never touched turf; against Sweden he arced a header so late it felt like an after-credit scene. Yet his influence reached beyond the scoreline. Room-mate Zinho recalls midnight corridor debates where the striker lectured teammates on sleep cycles: "Eu durmo quando a bola dorme." I sleep when the ball sleeps.

After the semi-final, Parreira offered to substitute Romário to preserve stamina. The response—"ME TIRA E EU TE MATO"—needed no translation. Brazil eked past the United States, then the Dutch, and finally faced Italy beneath Pasadena's rose-bled sky. One hundred twenty minutes of chess ended 0-0; the shoot-out opened with Romário glancing at Gianluca Pagliuca, nodding a private promise, and stroking home. Roberto Baggio's miss later sealed Brazil's fourth star; Romário accepted the Golden Ball wearing socks rolled to the ankle bone, smiling like a man who always knew the ending.

Back in Rio he party-hopped for forty-eight hours, telling reporters, "God made the sun so I could celebrate in daylight, too." Fans forgave the arrogance; to them it felt like agency after years of beautiful failure.

Act II   Baton Pass to a Meteor (1996-97)

Just as Romário's shadow stretched longest, a teenager from São Cristóvão named **Ronaldo** burst through it. PSV Eindhoven had polished Ronaldo's raw ore into European gold; Barcelona's FENÓMENO season of 1996-97 confirmed a generational vault. Romário, never shy, sniffed that "the kid will be great—when I retire." Ronaldo replied with 47 goals, a Puskás-grade solo against Compostela, and an easy grin that sold pastel T-shirts by the container.

Parreira's successor, Mário Zagallo, tried fitting both Rs into the same XI at Copa América '97. Training-ground witnesses recall Romário arriving late in flip-flops, Ronaldo arriving early with GPS-age heart-rate monitors, and Zagallo mediating like a kindergarten teacher. The experiment scored goals but combusted over curfew violations, Nike-sponsored media events, and who got first dibs on free PlayStation kits. When Romário pulled a calf on the eve of France '98, many whispered karma.

Act III   The Night of the Convulsion (France 1998)

The 1998 squad, now built around Ronaldo and Rivaldo—who had muscled past Juninho to claim the creative left channel—swept to the final. Then came July 12th, Saint-Denis. Hours before kickoff Ronaldo collapsed in the Château de Grande Roma hotel, body shuddering on tiled floor. Fellow striker Edmundo screamed; César Sampaio prised open clenched jaws to prevent tongue swallow; team doctor Lídio Toledo injected calm but not clarity. Ronaldo later described waking in hospital disoriented, begging to play despite medical advice.

The dressing room vibrated with superstition: television sets switched off to avoid evil-eye replays; Rivaldo prayed quietly; Zagallo wept into a towel. Doctors cleared Ronaldo ninety minutes before kickoff; many teammates swear his eyes stayed glassy. France needed no second invitation: Zidane headed two goals, Emmanuel Petit iced a third, and Brazil's dynasty crumpled 3-0. Conspiracy theories—corporate pressure, hidden seizures, Romário voodoo—flooded Brazilian tabloids. Ronaldo spent a week avoiding mirrors; Rivaldo walked Copacabana at 3 a.m. muttering scriptures; Zagallo resigned to a headline that read "The King Is Dead—Long Live Fear".

Act IV   Rivaldo's Lonely Genius

Between 1999 and 2001 Rivaldo became the most prolific Brazilian in Europe—La Liga titles, a Ballon d'Or, and a Camp Nou bicycle-kick hat-trick so audacious it triggered Richter tremors around Les Corts. Yet his national-team image blurred after a theatrical collapse against Turkey in Korea/Japan 2002. Struck on the thigh by a ball, Rivaldo clutched his face; FIFA fined him £4,500, Brazilian senators debated "ethical education," and Turkish fans burnt effigies. Rivaldo responded with goals against Belgium and England, each celebration finger to lips—a genius asking for library hush inside a carnival.

Act V Redemption in Yokohama (2002)

Luiz Felipe Scolari, gruff as farm fencing, inherited a wounded Ronaldo, a brooding Rivaldo, and a teenage Ronaldinho hungry for spotlight. His tactic was simple: two holding mids, three assassins, zero apologies. Ronaldo shaved a semi-circle into his hair to divert media from a swollen ankle; the haircut became a playground fad within 24 hours. He scored eight goals, including a semifinal brace that silenced Turkey's revenge chant and a final double against Germany that crowned him Golden Shoe—and redeemed his 1998 ghost.

In those ninety minutes Ronaldo sprinted, paused, and finished like a man exorcising four years of static. Rivaldo assisted the opener by letting the ball roll between his legs— a feint so serene Kahn froze into statuary; moments later he dummied again, inviting Ronaldo's right foot to slam immortality. Brazil 2, Germany 0: the Rs had closed their circle.

Locker-Room Echoes

RONALDO ON 1998: "The seizure did not scare me. The idea of watching my brothers play without me—THAT is fear."
RIVALDO ON CRITICISM: "If I must choose between applause and the goal net, I choose the net. The net never forgets."
ROMÁRIO, WATCHING 2002 FROM A RIO BAR: "I taught the boy to finish; good students always surpass the teacher."

Epilogue: Three Signatures, One Legacy

Romário wrote the blueprint for ruthlessness, Ronaldo grafted resilience onto spectacle, and Rivaldo blended mathematics with melancholy. Their intertwined stories taught Brazil that ego can be asset and anchor, that catastrophe may pre-sketch renaissance, and that football scripts rarely end where they begin. The Rs did not always share space harmoniously—one stole minutes, another headlines—but together they dragged the Seleção from pragmatic drought through traumatic storm and into technicolour sunrise.

Their legacy lives in every Brazilian striker who trains finishing drills at dawn, chasing the one-touch authority of Romário; in every sports-psych worksheet citing Ronaldo's seizure as case study in crisis response; in every VAR review reminding fans of Rivaldo's Oscar-winning shin-face flop. Three letters, three careers, one decade that shaped modern Brazil—proof that even in a team game, individual meteors can rechart the constellations.

Chapter 16   The Diaspora XI: Exporting Talent to Every League

At 2:47 a.m. on a muggy October night in 2003, a flight clerk at São Paulo's Congonhas Airport clicked a counter and tallied his twentieth footballer departure of the week. Teenagers in nylon tracksuits, duffel bags heavy with cleats and prayer cards, waited in line for redeyes to Kyiv, Porto, Eindhoven, Tokyo. No entourage, no press—just hopeful silhouettes under strip-lighting, trading WhatsApp hugs with mothers clutching travel biscuits wrapped in tinfoil. If you counted their agents and whispered promises, the terminal resembled an invisible stadium, one preparing to field a full XI across every hemisphere.

By the early 2000s, Brazil had become not just an exporter of grain and iron ore, but of human footballing capital. In 2001, there were approximately 500 registered Brazilian players abroad. By 2008, FIFA estimated nearly 1,200—a tidal surge that recast the nation's relationship with its most beloved game. JOGA BONITO still bloomed, but it now often flowered in borrowed soil.

Seeds of Migration

Economic stagnation, mismanaged domestic leagues, and volatile currency forced clubs to monetize talent earlier. Where Pelé and Garrincha had once stayed in Brazil for prime years, stars of the 2000s left at 16 or 17. Transfer fees—lucrative even after agent cuts—bankrolled decrepit training grounds, cleared tax debts, and kept club presidents afloat through re-election cycles.

Scouts flooded youth tournaments like the Copa São Paulo de Juniores, waving contracts in Portuguese, Spanish, Italian. Clubs like Shakhtar Donetsk, Ajax, and CSKA Moscow developed Brazilian pipelines—less buying finished idols, more cultivating rough diamonds they could polish, then resell at UEFA mark-ups.

A single week at the 2005 São Paulo Cup saw twenty-five players sign pre-contracts with European or Asian clubs. At times the scramble resembled open-market trading: handshakes made in car parks, contracts signed in hotel lobbies.

Third-Party Ownership: The Shadow Brokers

With clubs desperate for upfront cash and players unwilling to wait for big-stage validation, an ecosystem of "third-party owners" emerged. Private investors purchased slices of players' future rights—10 percent here, 40 percent there— like venture capitalists buying startup equity.

The 2000s transfer landscape bristled with backroom arrangements: a Brazilian teenager registered with a minor club would be "sold" to an investment group, who then brokered a larger sale to Europe, pocketing the difference. Clubs like Desportivo Brasil and Rentistas in Uruguay became waystations more than teams.

FIFA only banned third-party ownership in 2015, but by then dozens of careers had already been routed through murky channels. Corinthians' controversial deal for Argentine Carlos Tevez in 2005, brokered by Media Sports Investment (MSI), shone a global spotlight on these operations—but for many lesser-known Brazilians, third-party deals were the only ticket out.

As agent Wagner Ribeiro infamously put it: "The Brazilian dream today is not the Seleção—it's the stamp on the passport."

The Geography of the Diaspora

By 2010, Brazilian players dotted the footballing globe:

- **Ukraine**: Shakhtar Donetsk fielded a half-Brazilian starting XI—Fernandinho, Willian, Douglas Costa among them—adapting flair to frozen pitches.

- **Japan**: J.League squads like Kashima Antlers and Kawasaki Frontale signed compact, versatile attackers like Marquinhos and Danilo, marrying GINGA to disciplined pressing.

- **Russia**: Vágner Love became a cult hero at CSKA Moscow, his blue-dyed hair and samba celebrations thawing Muscovite winters.

- **Middle East**: Oil-rich clubs offered six-figure monthly salaries to players barely old enough to rent cars elsewhere.

- **China**: In a new frontier, players like Elkeson and Paulinho rebranded as local stars, some even naturalizing for World Cup bids.

Each migration reshaped both the host club and the traveler. Brazilian wingers learned to time runs to Scandinavian crosswinds; midfielders calibrated slide-tackles to Russian snow. Hybrids emerged: technically gifted, tactically drilled, culturally amphibious.

Midnight Farewells

Journalists began chronicling the surreal rituals of departures: agents booking tickets at midnight to avoid press leaks; mothers sneaking good-luck charms into sons' carry-ons; farewells punctuated by teary churrasco dinners and promises to wire back euros by Christmas.

One agent, asked why flights always departed so late, grinned: "Dreams ride the night shift."

In 2006, a 17-year-old midfielder from Salvador kissed the forehead of his grandmother outside Terminal 2 and boarded a flight to Rotterdam. Years later, that boy—Douglas Costa—would sprint past German defenders wearing Bayern Munich red, every stride an echo of that humid night.

Case Study: Shakhtar's Samba Pipeline

Perhaps no club symbolized the diaspora better than Shakhtar Donetsk under Romanian coach Mircea Lucescu. Starting in 2004, Shakhtar signed waves of young Brazilians— Matuzalém, Ilsinho, Jadson—offering high salaries, Champions League exposure, and patient tactical schooling.

The Donbass experiment paid off: Shakhtar won the 2009 UEFA Cup with six Brazilians starting the final. Fernandinho's rise from Curitiba teenager to Manchester City pivot owed much to the cold nights under Lucescu's stern tuition.

Yet interviews revealed homesickness too: players imported Brazilian chefs, hosted clandestine pagode parties, Skyped family dinners across eight time zones. The grass underfoot stayed icy; the music in headphones stayed tropical.

The Double-Edged Sword: Talent Drain vs. Remittance Renaissance

Critics lamented that exporting teenagers weakened domestic leagues. Legendary commentator Galvão Bueno mourned during a 2007 broadcast: "Our BRASILEIRÃO is becoming a window, not a cathedral."

But remittances told another story. Young players sent millions back to hometowns, financing house builds, college tuition for siblings, even entire community pitches. Economic geographers called it the "Futebol Remittance Cycle"—

football as both cultural export and social leveller.

Still, the cost was clear: fans grew up idolizing stars glimpsed only through European streams; hometown allegiances fractured along offshore club lines; grassroots dreams shifted subtly from Maracanã to Mestalla, from Pacaembu to Parc des Princes.

Cultural Blending and Tactical Evolution

The diaspora created cross-pollination. Brazilian attackers absorbed German gegenpressing, Italian zonal marking, Dutch positional play. When they returned to the Seleção, they brought those languages back in their boots.

Brazil's 2002, 2010, and 2014 teams reflected this hybridization: less samba freeform, more choreographed percussion. Neymar's tactical schooling under Luis Enrique, Casemiro's midfield anchoring learned at Real Madrid— each bore diaspora fingerprints.

Meanwhile, European clubs increasingly styled their recruitment around BRAZILIANITY—seeking players who could DANCE INSIDE DISCIPLINE, who could improvise within systems.

The Emotional Tax

Not every departure glittered. Players like Kerlon—he of the famous "seal dribble"—vanished into injury and obscurity after stints in Russia and Japan. Youngsters barely out of adolescence struggled with loneliness, racial prejudice, and career burnout.

A 2015 FIFPro survey found Brazilian migrants among the most likely to suffer depression linked to unstable contracts abroad. One poignant diary, later published anonymously, recorded:

"THE BALL MOVES FAST HERE, BUT LONELINESS MOVES FASTER."

The Diaspora XI: A Thought Experiment

Imagine fielding a team composed entirely of Brazilian exports:

- **GK**: Júlio César (Inter Milan)

- **RB**: Maicon (Roma)

- **CBs**: Thiago Silva (PSG), Lúcio (Bayern)

- **LB**: Marcelo (Real Madrid)

- **DMs**: Fernandinho (Man City), Paulinho (Guangzhou)

- **AM**: Oscar (Shanghai SIPG)

- **Forwards**: Hulk (Zenit), Alexandre Pato (Milan), Vágner Love (CSKA Moscow)

A team trained on red-eye flights, Agent-deals, Skype calls, and the bittersweet prayer that someday they'd come home to a nation still dreaming through their borrowed glories.

Closing Whistle

Brazil's football diaspora is not just a matter of numbers but of feeling: a mingled pride and ache, a reminder that FUTEBOL belongs both to the beach and the boarding gate. Every 17-year-old chasing a European signature carries not just cleats and ambition, but the invisible cargo of samba, salt air, and late-night street-lamp matches tucked into their duffel bags.

They leave at midnight; they call back at dawn. In between, somewhere over an ocean, the game rewrites them—and Brazil along with it.

Chapter 17　Futsal—The Hidden Classroom

It begins in a school gymnasium no wider than a bus depot, fluorescent lights buzzing overhead, dust motes swirling with every shuffle of sneakers. Five-a-side, no walls, no time to breathe. The ball, stitched leather over a rubber bladder, barely bounces. There are no throw-ins; the game spits the ball back into play through kick-ins or deft side-rolls. Possession is currency. Hesitation is suicide. Here, on varnished hardwood and concrete courts from Recife to Porto Alegre, Brazilian footballers learn lessons that no sprawling grass pitch could teach.

By the time Pelé made his Santos debut, he had logged more hours on futsal courts than full-sized fields. Ronaldinho juggled futsal balls barefoot on Porto Alegre's south side, learning to shield with hips and eyes. Neymar's first stepovers echoed in the echo chambers of São Vicente's municipal gym. Futsal—the **hidden classroom**—gave Brazilian players the instincts that TV highlights later called magic.

The Invention of a Pressure Cooker

Futsal (or FUTEBOL DE SALÃO) formalized in 1930s Uruguay, born of basketball courts repurposed for rainy days. Brazilians quickly adapted the game, producing their own rules emphasizing low-bounce balls and court-bound tempo. By the 1950s, São Paulo staged national tournaments; by the 1970s, futsal federations rivaled eleven-a-side for youth participation numbers.

A futsal ball is roughly 30% heavier than a standard football and half as lively off the surface. It demands not just touch but **calculated cushioning**. Coaches call it TEMPO NO TOQUE—timing in the touch. Instead of racing onto balls in space, players learn to collect under pressure, pivot in phone booths, and disguise passes with shoulder feints rather than acres of grass.

Learning to See: Peripheral Vision and Speed of Thought

Scientific studies affirm what playground coaches long knew: futsal players make more decisions per minute than their grass-bound peers. A 2017 JOURNAL OF SPORTS SCIENCE study found futsal players averaged **more than double** the technical actions per minute compared to 11-a-side counterparts. More touches, more decisions, more rapid-fire feedback loops.

Thiago Alcântara, raised in Brazil before transferring to Barcelona's academy, credits futsal for developing his trademark no-look passes: "YOU DON'T GLANCE WIDE IN FUTSAL—YOU FEEL WIDE." Similarly, Philippe Coutinho credits futsal for the half-second pre-snap vision that allowed him to thread impossible Liverpool passes through crowds.

In futsal, there's no hiding behind systems. A winger doesn't just track back—they rotate into defensive zones without prompting. A pivot striker must also double as a first-line presser. Thus players develop **global awareness**, not just positional literacy.

Coaches Unlocking the Code

Modern managers increasingly mine futsal for tactical solutions. Pep Guardiola, obsessed with tight-space rondos, built Barcelona's tiki-taka around futsal principles: numerical overloads, split-second wall passes, third-man runs.

Jürgen Klopp's Liverpool employed futsal-specific drills in tight quadrants to simulate pressing traps. In Brazil itself, youth coaches like André Bié of Corinthians' futsal division preach that **creativity is a survival skill**, not a luxury: "FUTSAL FORCES PROBLEMS EVERY SECOND—WHOEVER SOLVES FASTEST, WINS."

Santos FC's youth academy built miniature courts adjacent to standard pitches, so players like Rodrygo and Kaio Jorge could alternate surfaces between sessions. RITMO CURTO (short rhythm) became as vital as 30-yard crossfield switches.

From Gym Rats to Global Icons

The player roster crediting futsal reads like a FIFA gala seating chart:

- **Pelé** – "Futsal made me sharper; you don't get to think—you react."

- **Ronaldinho** – "My dribbles are futsal dribbles stretched onto grass."

- **Neymar** – "Futsal is poetry—you rhyme without space."

- **Ronaldo** – "In futsal you are always marked. You dance or you die."

- **Coutinho** – "The wall pass—PAREDINHA—is a futsal gift I use every match."

Even non-Brazilians like Lionel Messi and Andrés Iniesta cut their teeth on futsal courts, adapting its tempo to wider fields.

Futsal's Tactical Echo

Beyond individual skills, futsal tactics reverberate at macro level:

- **Rotations**: Players interchange spontaneously to confuse man-markers.

- **Third-Man Principle**: Every pass receiver sets up a third runner.

- **Exit Passes**: Quick one-two patterns escape pressure traps.

- **High Defensive Line**: Immediate swarming of ball-carriers after turnovers.

At the 2002 and 2010 World Cups, Brazilian full-backs overlapped as if conducting futsal shifts, generating mismatches through speed and layering rather than brute strength.

Even defensive midfielders like Casemiro, schooled on São Paulo courts, used futsal habits: tackle, lift head, find outlet pass within two seconds. Delay was death.

Why the Court Builds Joy

Grass can flatter athleticism; futsal flatters intellect. Without space, fantasy is compressed into centimetres. Improvisation blooms not from idle flair but necessity.

Sociologist Gilmar Mascarenhas argued that futsal imprints a "**culture of gambiarra**"—the Brazilian knack for improvised solutions—onto players' bodies. Elastic ankles, roll-drags, pivot flicks: all born under claustrophobic duress.

The joy fans see in Brazilian flicks, no-looks, and scoop-passes is joy compressed, forged on varnish courts with goalposts made from stacked chairs.

Futsal and the Future

Professional futsal now boasts its own FIFA World Cup, multi-million sponsorships, and Brazilian stars like Falcão and Rodrigo who chose court glory over grass fame. Yet in favelas and suburb gyms, the old educational role endures.

Top clubs integrate futsal hours into U-13 and U-15 programs. Coaches rotate small-sided games through sand, futsal, and grass to cross-pollinate movement patterns. The CBF mandates futsal experience as a curriculum requirement for youth licensing.

A teenager in Fortaleza dribbling through fluorescent glare today may be tomorrow's playmaker at the Bernabéu. His first moves—the pirouette through two defenders, the sole-roll to escape a trap—owe less to sprawling fields than to tight courts where the only way out was art.

Epilogue: The Gym that Never Empties

At midnight, in a neighborhood gym in São Paulo's Capão Redondo district, ten teenagers play a futsal match under cracked ceiling fans. No scouts watch, no trophies await. But every blind pass, every elastic flick, every escape under pressure stitches another thread into Brazil's football tapestry.

When you see a Brazilian winger nutmeg two defenders and scoop the ball over a keeper, remember: it started here. In the hidden classroom. In the rattling sneakers. In the echoing whistle of a coach reminding kids that if you can dance inside a box, you can dazzle on a world stage.

The court is small. The dreams it forges are infinite.

Chapter 18   The Other Seleção: Marta and the Rise of the Women's Game

At dawn in Dois Riachos, Alagoas, the air smells of cane sugar and red clay. The town's dirt fields, rutted by goat hooves and motorcycle tracks, have no nets and few lines. Yet on one of those patches, a barefoot girl named Marta Vieira da Silva spent her mornings juggling a deflated ball, one touch for each of her hopes: escape, dignity, a chance to play.

In a country where boys who dazzled with a football were called CRAQUES and girls were called foolish, Marta's dream felt heavier than the ball itself. It would take decades, torn sneakers, borrowed jerseys, and legislative fights before Brazil's women's football would rise onto the same global stage as the men's. Marta became the brightest light of a movement born not from system but in spite of it—a Seleção that fought to exist before it could dare to win.

Forbidden Games: A Law Against Women's Football

For thirty-eight years, Brazil literally outlawed women from playing football. In 1941, under the Vargas regime, **Decree-Law 3,199** stated that "women shall not engage in sports incompatible with the conditions of their nature," listing football, rugby, polo, and boxing among the banned activities. Pseudoscientific arguments claimed football would damage reproductive organs; newspapers derided women who wanted to play as "masculinized."

Unofficial matches continued in favelas and sugar-cane towns, away from police eyes. Girls played barefoot, often chased off pitches by boys or adults enforcing "tradition." Marta's mother, Dona Tereza, recalls hiding Marta's tattered football behind the stove so neighbours wouldn't report them.

The ban was only officially repealed in 1979, yet even then, the sport received no institutional support. No leagues, no funding, no visibility. Brazil had decriminalized women's football without dignifying it.

Sugar Fields and Torn Sneakers: Marta's Early Life

Born in 1986, Marta grew up in an Alagoas where "football was a boy's birthright and a girl's burden," as one journalist wrote. Her first balls were plastic grocery bags wrapped in string. When she showed up at neighborhood games, older boys tried to chase her off; after she nutmegged two defenders in a row, they argued over whose team would "have to" take her.

By age fourteen, Marta's skills turned heads beyond the cane fields. A scout from Vasco da Gama spotted her and offered a lifeline: a bus ticket to Rio, a bunk bed in a crumbling dormitory, and a slot on a fledgling women's squad with no guarantee of salary. Marta accepted. She boarded a greyhound carrying a rucksack and a dream larger than any field she had seen.

Her diary from that time, later published, carried a single line repeated three times: "VOU JOGAR. VOU JOGAR. VOU JOGAR." I will play.

The Slow Rise: Institutional Indifference and Player Perseverance

The early 2000s saw Brazil's women's national team exist almost by accident. Uniforms were hand-me-downs from youth men's squads; training camps often canceled for lack of funds. Players like Sissi, Pretinha, and Roseli paid their own airfare to tournaments.

Despite the neglect, talent flowered. In 1996, Brazil fielded a women's team at the Atlanta Olympics, finishing a surprising fourth. FIFA finally staged its second Women's World Cup in 1999, and Brazil reached the semifinals, with Sissi's curling free kicks and heart-out performances shocking the organizers who hadn't even thought to televise the group stage in Brazil.

Marta entered the national consciousness at 17, dazzling defenders at the 2003 World Cup in the United States. Observers described her as "a left foot wrapped in laughter," "the phantom of the wing," and "the smile that nutmegged the patriarchy."

Six Awards, One Message

Marta won her first FIFA World Player of the Year award in 2006. She won again in 2007. And 2008. And 2009. And 2010. Then, after a decade in the crucible, again in 2018.

In every acceptance speech, Marta steered the camera away from herself toward the young girls watching. In 2018, with mascara streaming down her cheeks, she said: "BELIEVE. IT'S NOT JUST ABOUT HAVING A BALL AT YOUR FEET. IT'S ABOUT HAVING DREAMS IN YOUR HEART."

Her club career soared as well. Stints in Sweden (Umeå IK), the United States (FC Gold Pride, Orlando Pride), and a brief flirtation with European giants expanded her audience. Yet even at peak fame, Marta never disowned the struggles: when sponsors asked her to shoot glamorous ads, she insisted on including scenes of dirt pitches and handmade balls.

The Policy Turn: CBF's Late Awakening

Under growing pressure, the Brazilian Football Confederation (CBF) finally began investing in women's football in the mid-2010s. Key moves included:

- Requiring top-flight men's clubs to field women's teams as a licensing condition.

- Launching a professional Campeonato Brasileiro Feminino in 2013.

- Hiring Pia Sundhage, a world-class coach, to lead the women's national team.

- Setting minimum wage floors for professional women players in the domestic league.

Results followed slowly but surely. São Paulo FC, Corinthians, and Santos built strong women's programs. Attendance records broke for domestic finals. TV Globo, long reluctant, agreed to air women's national team matches in prime-time slots during Copa América Feminina.

Marta herself welcomed the changes but warned: "SUPPORT CANNOT ARRIVE ONLY WHEN THE MEDALS GLITTER. IT MUST ARRIVE IN THE MUD, IN THE HARD PLACES, WHERE THE NEXT MARTAS WAIT."

Locker-Room Chronicles

From player interviews and documentaries, vivid stories emerge:

- Formiga, who debuted for Brazil in 1995 at age 17, said she sometimes received only two training shirts for an entire year.

- Cristiane, Marta's longtime teammate, recalled eating dry pasta before matches because the hotel couldn't arrange proper meals for the women's squad.

- At the 2007 World Cup in China, Marta and teammates hand-stitched the Brazilian flag onto their travel jackets because their federation-issued gear had no women's version.

Even so, Marta led Brazil to Olympic silver in 2004 and 2008, a World Cup final in 2007, and semi-final finishes that made samba songs and documentary titles.

A New Generation: Standing on Marta's Shoulders

Debinha, Geyse Ferreira, Adriana, Ary Borges—today's rising stars owe debts to the trail Marta carved. They dribble faster, shoot harder, and sign sponsorship deals once unimaginable for women in Brazil. The JOGO BONITO is no longer confined to men's turf.

Grassroots initiatives exploded: projects like Guerreiras Project, Meninas em Campo, and A Seleção Feminina have turned futsal courts and schoolyards into incubators for a more inclusive future.

At the 2019 World Cup in France, young girls in São Paulo wore Marta jerseys with pride once reserved for Pelé or Neymar. An eight-year-old at Ibirapuera Park wore a handmade sign: "EU SOU MARTA DE AMANHÃ." I am tomorrow's Marta.

Marta's Final Whistle

Approaching her fortieth birthday, Marta has hinted that her next World Cup will be her last. Yet she refuses to frame her legacy as farewell.

"I WANT MY DEPARTURE TO BE A BEGINNING, NOT AN ENDING. I WANT EVERY GIRL TO KNOW THE FIELD IS HERS, TOO."

Already, the other Seleção—the women's Seleção—is no longer a curiosity. It is a force, a rhythm, a movement surging beyond sugarcane fields and cracked futsal courts into stadiums of thunderous applause.

The torn footballs have been patched. The clay has been lined. And Marta's footprints—bare, fierce, luminous—show the way forward.

Chapter 19 Concrete Colosseums: Stadiums, Architecture, and Fan Rituals

At 6:17 p.m. on a matchday in São Paulo, the air hums with a frequency no instrument can tune. It is the collective shiver of tens of thousands crossing turnstiles, stomping concourses, swaying banners, drumming, praying, laughing, weeping—all at once. You feel it before you hear it, a low subsonic growl that rises through concrete ribs and reverberates against the floodlights. The stadium is not merely built; it is inhabited, animated, electrified. Bricks and mortar become living muscle.

Brazilian football's cathedrals tell a parallel story to the game itself: from rickety wooden bleachers to monumental mega-arenas, from handmade goalposts to acoustic-optimized bowls where every chorus ricochets like gospel. This is the tale of how Brazil poured football's soul into concrete—and how matchday rituals turned architecture into liturgy.

Wood and Hope: The Early Grounds

At the start of the 20th century, Brazil's first pitches were little more than cricket fields repurposed for new passions. São Paulo's Velódromo, built in 1901 for cycling, hosted football matches atop a haphazard mix of grass and sand. Bleachers consisted of splintering planks nailed onto lopsided frames. Goals used telephone poles for uprights.

Still, fans flocked. Fluminense's early matches at Laranjeiras field drew Rio's elite in starched collars and parasols, the crowd leaning over rope barriers to catch a glimpse of the new English export. A sense of spectacle began to form: picnics on the touchline, marching bands at halftime.

But as the crowds thickened, Brazil needed sturdier shrines.

Concrete Dreams: Stadiums of the 1930s–1950s

The first true Brazilian stadiums—Vila Belmiro in Santos, Estádio das Laranjeiras in Rio—used reinforced concrete to anchor the burgeoning sport into permanence. Architects borrowed ideas from bullrings and boxing arenas: close sight-lines, steep seating to compress sound.

Then came the grandest ambition yet: the Maracanã.

Commissioned for the 1950 World Cup, Rio's **Estádio Jornalista Mário Filho** was designed to hold 200,000 spectators—then the largest sporting venue on Earth. Its architects, Pedro Paulo Bastos and Rafael Galvão, envisioned a colossal oval with a continuous upper ring floating over the terraces like a halo.

More than an engineering marvel, the Maracanã was a social experiment. Tickets were priced from luxury boxes to general admission cement steps—**geral**—where the working class danced, drank, and sang in ceaseless waves. It was Brazil's first true concrete colosseum, a place where presidents and street vendors could celebrate or mourn shoulder to shoulder.

At the 1950 final, when Uruguay stunned Brazil, 200,000 voices collapsed into the infamous **Maracanazo** silence—a silence so vast it seemed etched into the cement itself.

Acoustic Alchemy

Stadium designers learned quickly: sound is architecture's secret ingredient.

The Maracanã's ring amplified chants, bouncing them in layered echoes. Pacaembu in São Paulo curved its grandstands to create natural reverb, turning modest drums into battlefield thunder.

Later, modern arenas like Mineirão in Belo Horizonte and Beira-Rio in Porto Alegre integrated even tighter acoustics: parabolic roofing, angled seats, gaps that let airflow feed drums without diluting them. Acoustics were no accident; they were the architecture of ecstasy.

When Corinthians fans belt out "TIMÃO, EÔ!" at Arena Corinthians, the song whips in three-second delays, layering ghost-choirs onto the living one.

Match-Day Rituals: From Firecrackers to Faith

Stadium rituals turned concrete into heartbeat:

- **Drums** (BATERIAS): Samba-school-trained drummers lead chants that ripple up concrete spines. At Maracanã, organized supporter groups like TORCIDA JOVEM DO FLAMENGO synchronize rhythms to cue entire sections' standing waves.

- **Paper Rains**: Fans at São Paulo's Morumbi Stadium throw shredded phone books (yes, actual books) over entrances when the teams take the field, creating snowstorms of white confetti that glint under floodlights.

- **Prayers and Superstitions**: At Allianz Parque, Palmeiras fans recite AVE MARIA en masse before kick-off. Some wear lucky jerseys never washed after victories.

- **Firecrackers** (FOGOS): Despite regulations, vendors outside grounds peddle fireworks that fans set off before, during, and after goals, shaking foundations like samba-scented earthquakes.

- **Banners and Mosaics**: Gigantic BANDEIRÕES—sometimes spanning an entire stand—unfurl at kickoff, depicting club heroes, saints, political messages.

Corinthians' 2012 Libertadores final featured a 400-meter banner reading "TIME DO POVO"—team of the people.

At these moments, bricks and concrete cease to matter. The stadium breathes as a single organism.

World Cup Upgrades and Growing Pains

Hosting the 2014 World Cup prompted a wave of stadium renovations and new builds, each aiming for FIFA-standard modernity: luxury boxes, padded seats, retractable roofs.

The Maracanã was gutted and reborn at a cost of $500 million, replacing much of its egalitarian geral with corporate hospitality suites. New stadiums like Arena Pernambuco and Arena da Amazônia dazzled but left painful footprints: huge costs, white-elephant usage in the years after.

Fans grumbled. They missed the crumbling cement where the poor roared, missed standing on steps where your thighs burned and your voice blended into the concrete itself.

In some corners, a backlash brewed. Supporters formed **Barrabrava** movements insisting on singing, standing, and drum-banging against the sterilization of the fan experience. "Concrete is not enough," one leader said. "You must pour soul into it."

Stadiums as Storytellers

Each concrete colosseum carries the scars and songs of generations:

- **Pacaembu** whispers of Pelé's record goal streaks and Corinthian democracy rallies.

- **Beira-Rio** hums with Internacional's historic 2006 Libertadores conquest.

- **Mineirão** bears both Cruzeiro's highest triumphs and the deep wound of Brazil's 1–7 collapse to Germany in 2014.

Even ghost stadiums like Maracanãzinho (the "Little Maracanã," once a futsal giant) retain their legends like stubborn moss on stone.

How Concrete Shapes Emotion

Sociologists argue that stadium design influences emotional flow:

- **Steepness of Seats**: The sharper the rake, the faster noise falls onto the field.

- **Enclosure**: Full rings foster inclusivity; open bowls fragment cheers.

- **Material Density**: Denser concrete produces deeper echoes, turning claps into cannon-fire.

- **Tunnels and Choke Points**: Narrow walkways before entrance ramps create "compression points," amplifying tension like a steam valve.

Thus, a goal at Maracanã **feels** different from one at Estádio Nacional in Brasília, even if the scoreboard says the same.

Concrete, built right, amplifies not just sight-lines but SOUL-LINES.

Epilogue: Concrete Hearts Beat On

Tonight, a young fan in Fortaleza climbs cracked steps to the last row, clutching a drum whose skin is patched with duct tape. She pounds a rhythm handed down by older brothers, now faded into ghost songs on the terraces. Her voice joins thousands, swelling through steel and dust and floodlights.

Beneath her sneakers, concrete trembles—not from earthquake or storm, but from thousands of hearts, hammering in sync.

Brazil's stadiums are not inert monuments. They are organisms, inhaling drums, exhaling dreams. Concrete gave them bones; fans gave them life.

Chapter 20   Goals and Golpes: Football under Dictators and Democracy

In a country where football often felt like religion, it was perhaps inevitable that politicians would try to claim the pulpit. No regime understood this better than Brazil's military dictatorship, which from 1964 to 1985 wrapped itself in the yellow jersey, paraded the Seleção's triumphs as proof of national greatness, and staged stadium spectacles as anesthetic for deeper wounds. Yet even amid the drumbeats of state-sponsored celebration, cracks formed—banners smuggled into stands, players who refused to bow, and goals that, despite everything, refused to obey political choreography.

The ball, it turned out, was more subversive than generals calculated. It spun through juntas and parliaments, coups and constitutions, always hinting that whatever tried to capture it could never quite hold it.

1964: The Coup and the Capture

When Brazil's generals toppled João Goulart's left-leaning government in 1964, they seized not only the ministries but also the mythologies. Football, already the country's unifying passion, became an official tool of nationalism. New slogans plastered stadium walls: "BRASIL: AME-O OU DEIXE-O."—Brazil: love it or leave it.

The dictatorship understood that a televised Pelé goal was more persuasive than a press conference. Football victories were woven into national propaganda campaigns, with generals portraying Brazil as a harmonious, efficient machine on and off the pitch.

The 1970 World Cup in Mexico became the apex of this fusion.

1970: Goals as Propaganda Weapons

Brazil's third World Cup triumph—led by Pelé, Tostão, Jairzinho, Rivellino, and Carlos Alberto—offered the dictatorship a golden narrative. President Emílio Garrastazu Médici, an avid football fan and fearsome authoritarian, seized the moment.

State-controlled media ran saturation coverage: every Seleção training session, every goal, every victory parade. Rádio Nacional received special transmission privileges; newspapers published government-drafted "analysis" pieces under the guise of sports journalism. When Brazil beat Italy 4-1 in the final, Médici declared it proof that Brazil's "revolution" had modernized and unified the country.

Privately, players bristled. Pelé later wrote that Médici's involvement "soiled" the pure joy of victory. Tostão admitted teammates debated refusing the White House-style reception arranged by Brasília but feared reprisals too strong to ignore.

The World Cup trophy itself toured the country by helicopter, sometimes landing unannounced in public squares where soldiers orchestrated applause with bayonets drawn.

Football had won, but not entirely freely.

Dissidence Behind the Drums

Even under censorship, dissent percolated. Some supporter groups devised coded chants. At Atlético Mineiro's matches, crowds would chant "DIRETAS JÁ!"—Direct elections now—drowned by drums but visible to those who listened.

Banners snuck into stadiums carried double meanings. A cloth painted "GOOL DA DEMOCRACIA" at a Botafogo match was confiscated by security forces; others simply shouted "BRASIL SIM, GENERAL NÃO!" before quickly folding the cloth away.

In São Paulo's Morumbi Stadium, undercover police patrolled the GERAL looking for singers whose verses drifted into anti-government slogans hidden inside football chants.

Players faced careful lines. Socrates, captain of the 1982 Seleção and a leader of Corinthians' internal democracy movement, wore black armbands during matches to symbolize solidarity with civil-rights protesters. Sócrates once said, "THE FIELD IS FREEDOM'S LAST STAND."

The Corinthians Democracy: A Team Becomes a Movement

Perhaps the boldest act of resistance came not from stadium stands but from a locker room.

In 1981, Corinthians players—led by Sócrates, Wladimir, Casagrande, and Zenon—initiated the **Democracia Corinthiana** movement. Players voted on decisions from tactics to meal times; they wore jerseys emblazoned with the word "Democracia."

More provocatively, they used matches as political platforms. Before the 1982 state championship final, Corinthians players entered the field carrying a banner: "GANHAR OU PERDER, MAS SEMPRE COM DEMOCRACIA."—Win or lose, but always with democracy.

State broadcasters tried to avoid televising the banner. Supporters waved homemade versions from the terraces. Civilian politicians, sensing the power of football's megaphone, began staging rallies outside stadiums.

Corinthians' victories that season felt like victories for democracy itself. When Diretas Já! (the mass movement for direct presidential elections) erupted in 1984, the stadiums served as crucibles of popular will.

Stadiums as Spaces of Control—and Resistance

The dictatorship's obsession with stadiums went beyond symbolism. Large venues allowed for mass surveillance. Ticket purchases were monitored; supporter groups infiltrated; public address systems could drown protests.

But stadiums also became some of the few remaining spaces where crowds could assemble, chant, and—for brief moments—outnumber their silencers. The dictatorship could script speeches, censor newspapers, and shutter universities, but it could not fully script the spontaneous roar after a 40-yard strike.

Football offered a strange, moving immunity.

Sociologist Roberto da Matta argued: "IN A DICTATORSHIP, THE STADIUM WAS PARADOXICALLY THE MOST DEMOCRATIC SPACE LEFT IN BRAZIL."

The Return to Civil Rule and Football's New Place

By the late 1980s, as Brazil staggered toward re-democratization, football's role shifted again. Now, players like Zico, Careca, and Romário expressed themselves more openly. The 1989 Copa América saw fans wear T-shirts reading "AGORA É NO VOTO!"—Now it's with votes!—as a rallying cry.

Footballers endorsed candidates, lobbied for youth investment, even sat in Congress. Romário would later serve multiple terms as a federal senator, campaigning on platforms of social justice and sports development.

Yet the commercialization of the game—accelerated by 1990s global marketing deals—also depoliticized football's popular spaces. Stadiums modernized, ticket prices rose, working-class terraces shrank. Spontaneous political chants became rarer, drowned by corporate anthems and choreographed T-shirt giveaways.

Football had helped build democracy—but democracy's market forces reshaped football.

Contemporary Echoes: Stadium Protests and the Ballot Box

In 2013, as Brazil prepared to host the 2014 World Cup, massive protests erupted—against corruption, against transit fare hikes, against stadium overspending. Once again, football stadiums became stages for discontent.

Fans at Maracanã matches unfurled banners reading "FIFA GO HOME!" and "HEALTH AND EDUCATION, NOT STADIUMS." Police clashed with demonstrators outside arenas. National television cut away from chants mid-broadcast.

Players, too, reawakened. Neymar posted support for protesters on social media. Dani Alves draped a protest scarf over his shoulders after scoring for Barcelona. The ball spun again, not under generals this time, but against the collusion of money and politics.

Goals that Outran Propaganda

Ultimately, Brazil's experience teaches that football is never truly apolitical, no matter how it is staged, sponsored, or censored. A goal may be claimed by presidents and generals—but the roar that greets it belongs to the people.

Pelé's header in 1970, Sócrates's backheel in 1982, Marta's tearful World Cup speech in 2019: these moments outlived their political wrappings, cutting through regimes and campaign slogans like songs echoing off concrete.

Football can be hijacked, yes. But the ball, mischievous and free, always rolls back to its rightful owners—the dreamers, the players, the crowds roaring in unison against any who would claim the game without understanding it.

Chapter 21   Factories of Dreams: Academies, Agents, and the Business of Talent

At 7:04 a.m. at Santos FC's **CT Rei Pelé**, the players are already wired. Heart-rate monitors beep. GPS vests map acceleration bursts. Biometric dashboards flash red or green under a trainer's thumb. The average age on the pitch is fifteen. To outsiders, it looks like a scrimmage. To insiders, it is a multi-million-dollar commodities exchange in motion—feet moving, futures rising.

Brazil once imagined footballers as street magicians sprung from beaches and back alleys. Now, increasingly, it manufactures them—through academies, scouts, biometric labs, and the sharp-eyed calculus of agents and clubs. Dreams remain. But they are measured, packaged, projected, sold. In the 21st century, Brazil's FÁBRICAS DE SONHOS—factories of dreams—run on data and hope in equal measure.

The Old Way: Luck and Dust

For most of the 20th century, a Brazilian footballer's journey began on sandlots and cobblestone alleys. Talent was spotted informally—by a neighbor, a coach, a cousin who "knew someone." Trials were brutal and largely unstructured: a handful of hopefuls sprinting, dribbling, juggling under a scout's squinting gaze. Documentation was optional. Contracts were handshake affairs, sometimes notarized with promises of a meal and a bus ticket.

Even the greats emerged this way: Garrincha discovered by chance at Botafogo; Romário recruited after scoring six goals in a beach tournament.

But as global football ballooned into a multi-billion dollar industry, informal networks proved too porous. European clubs wanted earlier access, tighter documentation, insurable assets. Brazil had to industrialize its dream-making—or risk losing the future.

Enter the Modern Academies

Top-flight clubs now invest millions in youth complexes designed to refine, monitor, and showcase talent.

Santos's Meninos da Vila (The Boys of the Village) became the prototype: a school that graduated Pelé, Neymar, Robinho, and Rodrygo across generations. Their method blends tradition and tech: barefoot futsal mornings to hone touch, followed by GPS-tracked sprint drills under sports scientists.

Flamengo's Ninho do Urubu—the Vulture's Nest—offers dormitories, classrooms, psych evaluations, nutrition labs. Players aged twelve to twenty sleep in bunk beds under Flamengo-themed quilts, study history and math by CBF curriculum standards, and spend afternoons in hyper-specified positional drills.

Clubs now track:

- VO2 max capacity by age fifteen

- Growth-plate scans to predict adult height

- Sleep cycles via wearable tech

- Stress hormone levels before tournaments

Each boy becomes a data point in an algorithm forecasting not only whether he can score today—but whether he can headline a Champions League final in 2029.

The Hidden Economy: Agents and Early Stakes

The earlier the identification, the sharper the agent's advantage.

Top talents now sign representation contracts at twelve or thirteen, often without fully understanding clauses. Parents, dazzled by dreams and desperate for security, sometimes sign rights away to agencies promising European trials or marketing deals.

Super-agents operate hybrid empires: part mentorship, part brokerage house. Rivaldo's agent managed his career like an investment portfolio; Neymar's early deals were structured through his father's agency, negotiating stakes across Santos, Barcelona, and later PSG.

A dark side lurks. FIFA has flagged cases where minors are "pre-sold" through labyrinthine third-party ownership schemes, with agents or investment groups claiming percentages of future transfer fees before players even turn professional.

Former CBF president Ricardo Teixeira once lamented, "WE ARE PRODUCING PLAYERS FASTER THAN WE CAN PROTECT THEM."

Biometric Dashboards and Talent Evaluation

Scouting now fuses eyeball tests with spreadsheet rows. Talent evaluators weigh:

- **Technical Index**: First touch, passing range, finishing under pressure

- **Tactical IQ**: Positional discipline, decision-making, scanning rates

- **Psychological Profile**: Resilience, adaptability, coachability

- **Athletic Potential**: Peak speed, agility ladder efficiency, injury predisposition

Leading clubs deploy platforms like Wyscout, Hudl, and STATSports to monitor U-17s as closely as seasoned pros. A teenager's hamstring elasticity at 15 could determine a €10 million transfer at 19.

Still, no model fully captures the unquantifiable: improvisation under stress, flair, instinct. Coaches call this the **Factor X**—the moment a boy, data be damned, does something so absurdly brilliant that spreadsheets crash under poetry.

Ethical Dilemmas: Dreams vs. Extraction

Brazil's football factories raise searing questions:

- **At what age should recruitment start?** Flamengo trials boys as young as nine. Critics warn of burnout and lost childhoods.

- **What about education?** Clubs provide schooling, but dropout rates spike once boys taste professional proximity.

- **What happens to the 90% who don't make it?** Some end up in semi-pro obscurity; others vanish from the system entirely, nursing shattered dreams.

- **Is export the goal?** Many academies explicitly groom players for European departure, with local fan bases rarely seeing them blossom.

In 2019, a fire at Flamengo's Ninho do Urubu tragically killed ten academy players, exposing lax safety standards and prompting national outrage. It served as brutal reminder: when dreams are industrialized, safeguarding must match ambition.

The Transfer Market: Brazil's Billion-Dollar Goldmine

Brazilian exports fuel the global transfer economy:

- Neymar's 2017 move to PSG: €222 million

- Vinícius Júnior to Real Madrid (2018): €45 million

- Rodrygo to Real Madrid (2019): €45 million

- Antony to Manchester United (2022): €95 million

In 2022 alone, Brazilian player transfers generated over €800 million worldwide. Brazil remains the world's top exporter of football talent, according to FIFA's Global Transfer Report.

Agents, clubs, and investors map scouting trips months in advance: looking for the next Gerson, the next Kaka, the next Neymar hiding among the Meninos da Vila or in futsal gyms along the Baixada Santista.

The Players' Perspective

For the boys inside the system, the journey is a tightrope between dream and pressure.

At São Paulo FC's Cotia academy, U-16 striker Gabriel once told a journalist: "MY FEET WANT TO DRIBBLE, BUT MY HEAD SAYS PASS. COACHES WATCH EVERYTHING." Another boy added: "MY DAD SAYS ONE INJURY AND IT'S BACK TO THE SUPERMARKET."

Stories of overnight riches dazzle—cars, gold chains, Instagram followers—but survivors whisper about loneliness in European hostels, homesickness in sub-zero Moscow, the whiplash from pampered academy life to foreign benches.

For every Rodrygo, a hundred teenagers ghost away from the dream factories, never spoken of again.

The Factory's Future

New technologies loom: AI-assisted scouting, machine-learning injury prediction, VR-simulated tactical drills. Brazilian academies scramble to adapt—partly inspired by European models, partly determined to retain their homegrown magic.

Some clubs have pivoted: Palmeiras and Grêmio invest heavily in mental health counselors for U-15 and U-17 squads. Others have linked education incentives to academy progression: finish your schooling, or forfeit your club stipend.

The dream factories keep humming, but the wiser ones now remember: a boy is not just a future balance sheet. He is a beating heart chasing an unpredictable ball toward a future no biometric dashboard can fully chart.

Closing Image: A Ball at Dawn

At 6:45 a.m., before the staff arrive at Santos's training complex, one boy, maybe twelve years old, sneaks onto the pitch, barefoot, ball tucked underarm. He juggles into the mist, the ball rising, falling, rising again, alone.

No agent yet. No data profile. No press kit.

Just a boy and a ball.

The oldest factory. The only one that ever truly mattered.

Chapter 22   Mineirão Meltdown: The 7-1 and a Nation's Mirror

It began with a silence so abrupt it was audible—the collective gasp of 58,141 inside the Estádio Mineirão, followed by an eerie vacuum, as if Belo Horizonte's humid night air had been sucked away. Five goals in twenty-nine minutes. Faces contorted into disbelief. Drums fell mute. Children cried. Men stared open-mouthed, unmoving. The scoreboard flickered: **Brazil 0–5 Germany**. Still twenty minutes to halftime.

By the final whistle, the numbers would etch themselves into infamy: Germany 7, Brazil 1. Not a defeat. Not even a humiliation. A disintegration, as if the entire mythology of Brazilian football—JOGO BONITO, samba rhythm, five-time champions—had crumpled into a pile of confused pixels.

But the match was not merely a footballing disaster. It became a national mirror, reflecting back systemic rot in governance, infrastructure, psychology, and pride. The ball merely exposed what politics, media, and daily life had tried for too long to wallpaper over.

Prelude: A Fragile House Built on Nostalgia

Brazil's 2014 World Cup hosting campaign had been a paradox from the start. Stadiums gleamed with billion-dollar renovations; airports modernized; FIFA executives proclaimed "spectacular readiness." Yet beyond the event's polished perimeter, street protests swelled. Citizens railed against public money diverted to World Cup projects while hospitals crumbled and schools leaked rainwater.

On the pitch, coach Luiz Felipe Scolari summoned the spirit of 2002: heart, aggression, collective GARRA (grit). Brazil's squad boasted Neymar's flickering genius, Thiago Silva's defensive leadership, and David Luiz's Hollywood charisma. Yet beneath the rallying cries of "A COPA É NOSSA!" cracks showed: midfield creativity was brittle; tactical plans reactive; psychological pressure volcanic.

Then Neymar fractured a vertebra against Colombia in the quarter-finals. Captain Thiago Silva picked up a suspension. Brazil limped into the semi-final against a German machine engineered with a decade's worth of tactical precision.

The Collapse: Goals, Stares, and Sobbed Anthems

The timeline reads like the black box of a disaster:

- **11th minute**: Thomas Müller unmarked at a corner, tap-in goal.

- **23rd minute**: Miroslav Klose breaks Ronaldo's World Cup scoring record—Brazilian fans barely boo.

- **24th, 26th, 29th minutes**: Kroos, Kroos again, then Khedira—all slicing through a Brazilian defense frozen by panic.

By 30 minutes, it was 5-0.

Julio César flapped at invisible crosses. David Luiz whirled with flailing desperation. Fernandinho disappeared. Oscar and Hulk wandered, shell-shocked.

German players, instructed pre-match to show respect, celebrated mutedly. Manuel Neuer later admitted: "WE DIDN'T KNOW HOW TO ACT AFTER THE FOURTH GOAL."

In the stands, tear-streaked faces became memes before the match ended: the boy clutching a replica trophy; the man covering his eyes with the Brazilian flag; the elderly woman mouthing "POR QUÊ?"—Why?

Social Media Firestorm

Within minutes, Twitter exploded:

- "Brazil has collapsed like a badly constructed stadium."

- "Germany scored faster than my internet loads in Rio."

- "Neymar is home. Brazil should join him."

The hashtag **#Mineiraço** (in homage to the 1950 MARACANAZO defeat) trended globally. WhatsApp groups flooded with gallows humor: cartoons of the Christ the Redeemer statue packing a suitcase, memes renaming Brazil as "South Germany."

Sociologists dubbed the meltdown "the first truly digital national trauma."

Post-Match Psychology: Debriefings and Tears

Brazilian Football Confederation psychologists ordered emergency group therapy sessions at the team hotel. According to leaked reports:

- Players broke down crying mid-sentence.

- Some blamed each other openly; others wept in exhausted silence.

- Scolari begged the players to "hold your heads up" before the third-place match—an appeal few believed.

Psychologists later diagnosed symptoms consistent with acute stress disorder. "It was grief without a funeral," said sports psychologist Regina Brandão, who advised the squad. "Not just for a match lost, but for a mythology shattered."

The Political Fallout

Protests reignited after the loss. Signs read:

- "THEY LIED ABOUT MORE THAN FOOTBALL."

- "OUR DEFEAT BEGAN WITH THE STADIUMS."

- "7-1 IS NOT THE WORST SCORE—IT'S OUR HEALTH SYSTEM."

Polls showed public trust in Dilma Rousseff's government plunging in the weeks following the semi-final, contributing to political turbulence that culminated in her impeachment two years later.

Football was not the cause of Brazil's systemic disillusionment—but it provided the perfect stage for its sudden, brutal unmasking.

Tactical Autopsy: How It Happened

Analysts peeled back the wreckage to find grim realities:

- **Naïveté**: Brazil pressed high but left their defensive midfield shredded. Fernandinho and Luiz Gustavo were swarmed by Germany's midfield rotations.

- **Mental Collapse**: After the second goal, positional discipline evaporated. Players chased ghosts rather than holding structure.

- **Tactical Hubris**: Scolari's reliance on emotional momentum over analytical preparation proved fatal against Germany's clinical ruthlessness.

- **Absence of Neymar and Silva**: Two key pillars missing—one creative, one defensive—exposed fragile tactical foundations.

Germany, by contrast, executed a masterclass in composure, positioning, and precision passing.

The margin—seven goals—was not exaggerated by luck. It was the cold mathematics of preparation versus nostalgia.

Cultural Reverberations

Songs were rewritten: carnival bands played parodies of national anthems with "7–1" refrains. T-shirts emerged: "KEEP CALM AND REMEMBER THE 7-1." Some bars renamed their "goal specials" to seven-shots-for-one-price offers.

At the same time, a darker edge crept in: xenophobic chants toward German tourists; graffiti reading "FIFA OUT, PRIDE IN."

Brazilians, famous for mocking their own defeats, struggled to find humor in this one.

As columnist Juca Kfouri wrote: "THE 7-1 IS NOT SIMPLY A SCORELINE. IT IS A SCAR."

Rebuilding from Ruins

In the aftermath:

- The CBF pledged technical revolutions—investing in futsal, coaching education, and mental preparation.

- Dunga was reappointed as national coach, symbolizing cautious pragmatism over spectacle.

- A new generation—Gabriel Jesus, Alisson, Marquinhos—emerged, determined to marry flair with tactical rigor.

- Veterans like Thiago Silva and Fernandinho carried permanent scars, struggling to erase the 7-1 ghost even after winning Copa América titles later.

Brazilian football still waltzed, but with a wary glance over its shoulder.

Epilogue: The Goal that Summed It All Up

In the 79th minute, Oscar broke through Germany's halfhearted backline and poked in a consolation goal. He didn't celebrate. Neither did the crowd.

It was not a goal. It was a whimper.

Seven to one. A number, a dirge, a reckoning.

In Brazil, the ball still spins, still invites dreams. But after July 8, 2014, it carries an extra weight: a reminder that passion without preparation, nostalgia without evolution, and pride without foundation eventually crumble.

The ball, merciless and democratic, rolls where the truth lies exposed.

Chapter 23   Recalibrating the Compass: Tite, Neymar, and the Search for Balance

At dawn on a cool August morning in Teresópolis, the training ground hums with low-key urgency. Cones and mini-goals are arranged in obsessive symmetry. Clipboards flash diagrams. The players file in—Marquinhos, Casemiro, Coutinho, Neymar—and immediately the rhythm begins: short passes, third-man runs, synchronized pressing triggers. Over it all, a steady voice directs, corrects, encourages. It belongs to **Adenor Leonardo Bacchi**, known to the world simply as **Tite**.

Brazilian football after the 7–1 collapse in 2014 resembled a compass spinning without north. Emotion had betrayed them; nostalgia had blinded them. Now Tite, equal parts professor and pastor, set out to realign Brazil's sense of footballing self: to marry European tactical rigor with the nation's eternal samba spirit. And standing at the center of this recalibration was the country's most dazzling, divisive star—**Neymar**—himself negotiating the crossroads between freedom and structure, art and order.

A Coach Forged in Humility

Tite's journey to the Seleção dug deep into Brazil's footballing soil. He coached for two decades across a half-dozen clubs, most famously building Corinthians into a winning machine—2011 Copa Libertadores champions, 2012 Club World Cup victors over Chelsea.

His coaching style married tactical modernity—4-1-4-1 pressing shapes, numerical overloads, defensive compactness—with a deep psychological sensitivity. Before matches, he recited quotes from SUN TZU and THE LITTLE PRINCE. He called players into his office not to berate, but to ask, "How's your mother? How's your sleep?"

He knew that in Brazil, football was not played from the mind alone, but from the stomach and the soul.

When Dunga's second tenure collapsed after the 2016 Copa América Centenario, the CBF turned, finally, to Tite—not for fireworks, but for foundation.

The Mission: Restore Identity Without Losing the World

Tite found a squad burdened with history and paralyzed by caution. His first commandment was simple: **play with joy, but anchored by structure**.

Training-ground changes were immediate:

- **Defensive Shape**: Two tight banks of four; fullbacks attacked selectively.

- **Positional Discipline**: Midfielders maintained vertical corridors; lateral freedom was conditional.

- **Rotational Triggers**: Players swapped roles based on ball position, a nod to European POSITIONAL PLAY concepts.

- **Mental Reset**: Players attended workshops with psychologists to address fear of failure post-7–1.

On the field, the effects were electrifying. Brazil won their first nine matches under Tite. Neymar thrived in a freer left-channel role. Gabriel Jesus emerged as a mobile No. 9. Coutinho lit fires between the lines. The team qualified for the 2018 World Cup atop South America's brutal CONMEBOL table by a thirteen-point margin.

The compass, it seemed, had found magnetic north again.

Neymar's Crossroads

At the heart of Tite's plan was Neymar—Brazil's avatar of genius, rebellion, fragility, and fame.

By 2016, Neymar had already conquered Barcelona's frontline alongside Messi and Suárez, winning a Champions League and global adulation. Yet personal frustrations festered: he wanted Ballon d'Or recognition, he wanted to step out of Messi's shadow.

In 2017, Neymar transferred to Paris Saint-Germain for a world-record €222 million. In PSG's glittering corridors, he became the face, the brand, the franchise.

But with it came fresh burdens: accusations of selfishness, diving theatrics, injury layoffs, nightclub headlines. In Brazil, public opinion divided sharply: **was Neymar the rightful heir to Pelé—or the symbol of a new, entitled generation?**

Tite knew he needed Neymar's brilliance—but contained within the team's structure. In closed-door meetings, he stressed:

- **Shared Responsibility**: Neymar was a "vertex" of the attack, not a "satellite" to be orbited.

- **Positional Integrity**: Dribble freely—but recover your shape after turnovers.

- **Emotional Management**: Channel provocations into productivity, not retaliation.

Tite gave Neymar tactical freedom in the final third—but demanded full buy-in to the team's compactness in transition. It was a delicate dance between leash and liberty.

Russia 2018: Beauty, Bruises, and Bitter Lessons

Brazil entered the 2018 World Cup with cautious optimism. In the group stages, Neymar's brilliance flickered: a late goal against Costa Rica, moments of magic against Serbia. Yet defensive shapes were tighter. Pressing traps sprang smoother. Brazil looked more European—but still recognizably Brazilian in spirit.

The Round of 16 against Mexico saw the best fusion: Neymar scored, assisted, pressed, grinned. Tite's vision seemed realized.

Then came Belgium in the quarter-finals. A high-tempo, counter-attacking Red Devils side exploited Brazil's defensive flanks. Neymar was closely marshalled. Casemiro's suspension exposed midfield vulnerability. Brazil's beautiful balance cracked—by inches, by missed rebounds, by inches of misjudged passes.

A 2–1 defeat. Respectable. Noble. Yet crushing.

Tite wept in the tunnel after the final whistle. Neymar left the field inconsolable, his face buried in his forearm.

Post-match analyses spoke less of tactical collapse, more of narrow margins. Brazil had not been outplayed; they had been edged.

Still, questions remained: could Brazil combine beauty and efficiency at the highest level, or would pragmatism forever dull their shine?

The Neymar Paradox Continues

Post-2018, Neymar's career continued along a seesaw:

- **Moments of Brilliance**: Champions League runs, acrobatic goals, outrageous assists.

- **Moments of Turbulence**: Injuries, missed international tournaments, accusations of indiscipline.

For Tite, managing Neymar meant managing contradiction: a player capable of divine intervention and self-sabotage within the same ninety minutes.

At the 2019 Copa América, Neymar's injury ruled him out; Brazil won without him, leaning on defensive solidity and Everton's emergent flair. Some pundits whispered that Brazil might be better without their capricious talisman.

But Tite refused that narrative. He saw Neymar's creative chaos as essential: "WE MUST NEVER KILL THE ARTIST INSIDE OUR SYSTEM," he told GLOBO ESPORTE.

The compass must point toward structure—but allow room for improvisation.

Training Ground Vignettes: The Balancing Act

Journalists embedded at Granja Comary training camps described scenes that captured Tite's philosophy:

- Neymar laughing as he nutmegged Marquinhos—but jogging back into shape immediately afterward.

- Coutinho and Paquetá drilled in three-second transition triggers after turnovers.

- Alisson Becker leading "silent" drills—no voices allowed, only positional signals.

- Dani Alves mentoring U-23 players on when to dribble and when to reset.

Discipline and joy. Freedom and rigor. The new Brazil would dance—but inside synchronized rhythms.

Toward Qatar 2022—and Beyond

In the run-up to the 2022 World Cup in Qatar, Tite's Brazil evolved further:

- A deeper squad rotation policy to avoid fatigue.

- Greater tactical fluidity—shifting between 4-2-3-1 and 4-3-3 mid-match.

- Young blood infusion: Vinícius Júnior's fearless wingplay; Antony's audacity; Raphinha's engine.

Neymar, at 30, matured into a deeper playmaking role, less pure sprinter, more conductor. His smile, subdued in Russia, began to widen again.

The quest was not just to win—but to win in a way that honored Brazil's footballing DNA.

Epilogue: The Compass Still Spins

Tite's tenure—regardless of final trophies—marked a profound recalibration. He proved that Brazil could play organized, disciplined, contemporary football without sacrificing soul.

And Neymar's journey mirrors the country's: brilliant yet burdened, free yet framed, always seeking the delicate line where beauty does not unravel into indulgence, where structure does not strangle genius.

The compass needle quivers still—not from confusion, but from a living, breathing balance.

It points not merely north or south, but to a dream: that the ball, when moving at its purest, needs no explanation. Only a rhythm. Only a dance. Only a heart beating to its own, unmistakably Brazilian drum.

Chapter 24 Gold at Home: The 2016 Olympic Redemption

The drums outside the Maracanã started three hours before kickoff, echoing across Rio's sultry August night. Inside the rebuilt stadium, tension coiled like a live wire. For all its World Cup glories, Copa América titles, and global fame, Brazil had never won men's Olympic football gold. Never. Not in Helsinki 1952. Not in Seoul 1988. Not even in London 2012, when a Neymar-led squad stumbled against Mexico.

Tonight, that burden—sixty-four years of unfinished business—hung over a new generation. On the opposite side of the tunnel waited Germany, the team whose seniors had inflicted the seismic 7–1 two years earlier. Here was symmetry. Here was the stage.

The whistle blew. Ninety minutes of tension and beauty unfolded. But destiny, as ever in Brazil, demanded drama—and delivered it through penalty shootouts, locker-room debates, and a soundtrack as chaotic and joyful as the nation itself.

The Ghosts of 2012 and 2014

To understand 2016's stakes, rewind:

In 2012, a Neymar-Oscar-Hulk front line dazzled all the way to the Olympic final—only to fall 2–1 to Mexico in a stunned Wembley. Neymar wept. Brazil wept harder.

In 2014, on home soil, the senior Seleção's historic collapse against Germany in the World Cup semifinal shattered national confidence. Banners at Rio's Sambadrome joked darkly: "WE DANCE BETTER THAN WE DEFEND."

Thus, the 2016 Olympic squad carried more than normal pressure. They were tasked with emotional repair— avenging ghosts, restoring belief, and finally filling the last gap on Brazil's footballing honors shelf.

Coach Rogério Micale, a softly spoken tactician, understood this. His approach: balance urgency with calm, tactical rigor with emotional freedom. And at the center of it all, the chosen captain: **Neymar da Silva Santos Júnior**.

Building the Squad: Stars, Kids, and Second Chances

Olympic squads are limited to U-23 players, with only three overage exemptions allowed. Brazil's choices:

- **Neymar**: Star, talisman, lightning rod.

- **Renato Augusto**: Midfield anchor with calm under fire.

- **Weverton**: Goalkeeper, seasoned but never capped at senior level.

Around them, a mix of rising talents: Gabriel Jesus, Gabriel "Gabigol" Barbosa, Marquinhos, Luan, Rodrigo Caio. Many would soon flood Europe's biggest clubs, but in August 2016, they were kids walking into a hurricane.

Training sessions at Granja Comary flickered between light-hearted rondos and ferocious tactical drills. Neymar led playlist battles—rotating from funk carioca to samba to Kendrick Lamar. Gabriel Jesus was teased for bringing only gospel tracks. Weverton, the oldest, chose silence before matches, a ritual respected by the teenagers around him.

Micale's mantra in every huddle: "OUR GOLD IS JOY WITH DISCIPLINE."

Group Stage Stumbles: Panic and Promise

Brazil's opening matches sparked anxiety:

- **0–0 vs. South Africa**: Static, anxious, Neymar muscled off the ball.

- **0–0 vs. Iraq**: Booed off the field by home fans at the Mane Garrincha Stadium.

Critics sharpened knives. Newspapers blared: "ANOTHER GENERATION, SAME COLLAPSE?"
In the locker room after the Iraq draw, Neymar reportedly slammed his boots into a trash can and shouted: "THEY FORGOT WHO WE ARE!"

Something cracked—in a good way.

Against Denmark in the third group match, Brazil finally exploded. A 4–0 masterclass, Neymar smiling wide again, Gabriel Jesus scoring twice, Marquinhos commanding the back line.

The dream was alive again—but the minefield only grew from there.

The Knockout Run: Rebuilding Confidence, One Dribble at a Time

- **Quarterfinal vs. Colombia**: A rugged, bruising 2–0 win, with Neymar absorbing endless kicks but delivering a glorious free-kick goal.

- **Semifinal vs. Honduras**: A cathartic 6–0 demolition. Neymar opened scoring within thirty seconds, the fastest goal in Olympic history. By final whistle, he lay flat on his back, arms outstretched, staring into the sunlit roof of the Maracanã.

The final loomed. Germany again. Destiny again.

This time, Brazil would not blink first.

Final Act: Maracanã, August 20, 2016

Brazil started brightly. In the 27th minute, Neymar stood over a free kick, 23 yards out. He struck it with that familiar, whip-crack curve. The ball kissed crossbar and net in one sonic boom. 1–0 Brazil. The stadium detonated in relief.

But Germany, machine-like, equalized through Max Meyer. 1–1. Anxiety seeped back. Extra time. Exhausted legs. Tightened throats.

Penalty shootout.

Locker-Room Strategy Session:
In the final team huddle before penalties, Micale quietly assigned kick-takers. Neymar insisted on taking the fifth—the closer's role. "If we win, I want it to be mine. If we lose, it must be mine too," he told his teammates.

Weverton, meanwhile, paced like a caged bull, whispering to goalkeeping coach Taffarel: "TODAY IS MINE."

The Penalties: Heartbeats on Parade

- **Germany first**: Goal.

- **Brazil**: Goal.

- **Germany**: Goal.

- **Brazil**: Goal.

- **Germany**: Goal.

- **Brazil**: Goal.

Then: Germany's Nils Petersen stepped up. Weverton guessed right. Saved.

The stadium trembled.

Neymar walked the long, lonely path to the penalty spot. He placed the ball. Paused. A breath that lasted a lifetime. A step. A caress. The net bulged.

Brazil 5, Germany 4.

Gold.

The Release: Tears, Drums, and Redemption

Neymar collapsed to his knees, sobbing. Teammates piled over him. From the rafters of the Maracanã, fireworks bloomed. Outside, on Avenida Atlântica, strangers embraced, car horns blared, firecrackers burst like champagne corks.

The Maracanã, so often a temple of heartbreak—from the 1950 Maracanazo to 2014's Mineiraço—became a cathedral of redemption.

Brazil, at last, had claimed Olympic gold.

Locker-Room Celebrations and Silent Prayers

Inside the dressing room:

- Neymar FaceTimed his mother, weeping: "WE DID IT, MÃE. WE DID IT."

- Gabriel Jesus and Gabigol danced barefoot on the lockers, blasting pagode from a Bluetooth speaker.

- Renato Augusto, the elder statesman, led a silent prayer circle. No speeches. Just joined hands and whispered gratitude.

Later, at the press conference, Neymar unpinned the captain's armband and declared he was stepping down from the role. "I've done my part," he said. "Let the next dreamers take over."

It was not resignation. It was release.

Epilogue: Beyond the Medal

Winning Olympic gold did more than fill a trophy cabinet. It stitched new faith into Brazilian football's battered psyche. It gave Neymar his coronation on home soil. It reminded a country bruised by economic crisis and political scandal that some promises could still be fulfilled.

And it proved, yet again, that Brazilian football—despite its dramas, collapses, and contradictions—remains, at its core, a story of resilience: boys and girls chasing impossible dreams across impossible odds until, at last, one net bulges and the heavens open.

Chapter 25   Spreadsheets Meet Samba: Data Analytics in the Seleção

At 9:02 a.m. inside the Granja Comary training complex, a flock of drones buzzes to life above the grass. Below, twenty yellow-shirted players shuttle between drills, tiny GPS pods sewn into their sports bras. On the sidelines, a laptop brigade watches in silence. One analyst mutters, "Casemiro's recovery range is up five percent." Another toggles a heat map showing Neymar's movement clusters.

This is not the football training of Garrincha's time—or even Romário's. This is the Seleção in the 21st century: where rhythm still rules, but spreadsheets translate the beat into ones and zeroes. Samba has met silicon. Instinct dances with algorithms.

And the outcome is an uneasy, evolving truce: a nation famous for improvisation now trying to codify genius without caging it.

The Traditional Model: Instinct Over Information

For most of Brazil's football history, analytics consisted of gut feelings and bar-stool debates. Coaches like Telê Santana trusted their eyes; players trusted the rhythms born of barefoot futsal and street corner pickup games.

Training journals might list simple metrics—number of sprints, goals scored in scrimmages—but there was no quantifiable tracking of distances covered, passing angles, or energy zones. Tactics were drawn on napkins, not software.

Brazilian football lived by the maxim: "QUEM SABE, SABE."—He who knows, knows. No need to measure magic.

But after the 7–1 trauma in 2014—and the tactical revolutions sweeping Europe—change became inevitable.

The Digital Turn: From GPS to Drones

Starting in 2015, the Brazilian Football Confederation (CBF) began a full-scale modernization of its analytics approach. Key innovations included:

- **GPS Vests**: All national-team players wear lightweight trackers measuring sprints, decelerations, heart rate, and "workload indices."

- **Drone Footage**: Overhead cameras capture entire tactical shapes during training, allowing coaches to freeze frames and show players real-time spacing errors.

- **AI Scouting Platforms**: Software like Wyscout, Hudl, and SciSports crunch hours of footage into digestible metrics—expected goals (xG), progressive passes, defensive actions.

At Granja Comary, data analysts now occupy as much floor space as physios. Every session generates gigabytes of information.

Sample Training Session:

- Players' top speeds flash in color-coded rankings.

- Pass completion under pressure is logged by quadrant.

- Heat maps show where transitions fail most often.

- Fatigue probability charts predict when subs will be needed in matches.

Translating Ginga: Can You Quantify Flair?

Brazil's biggest challenge is philosophical: how do you measure GINGA—the spontaneous body feint, the elastic change of rhythm, the no-look pass improvisation?

At first, analytics departments struggled. Standard metrics often penalized risk-taking:

- A flicked nutmeg attempt could count as a turnover.

- A long-range dribble could lower passing efficiency.

- A back-heel to a teammate who loses the ball looked worse than a safe sideways pass.

To address this, Brazilian analysts developed hybrid metrics:

- **Creativity Index**: Weighs risk vs. potential reward in attacking moves.

- **Pressure Evade Rate**: Measures successful dribbles under double or triple marking.

- **Unbalancing Actions**: Catalogues moves that cause defensive reshuffles, even without leading directly to goals.

Players like Neymar, Vinícius Júnior, and Raphinha rank higher in these bespoke categories than they would under traditional European models.

Still, some coaches worry that analytics culture risks blunting Brazil's historic freedom. Tite once warned in a press conference: "IF THE PLAYER ONLY PLAYS WHAT THE SPREADSHEET TELLS HIM, WE HAVE LOST OUR FOOTBALL."

Case Study: Brazil's 2019 Copa América Triumph

Brazil's data-driven renaissance bore fruit at the 2019 Copa América:

- Opponent tendencies were mapped via AI pattern recognition.

- Fitness loads were micromanaged to minimize injuries.

- Tactical drills incorporated "constraint-led learning"—forcing players into tight spaces to stimulate creative solutions under pressure.

Midfielder Arthur Melo explained: "WE WERE SHOWN DRONE FOOTAGE OF URUGUAY'S PRESSING PATTERNS. IT WAS LIKE PLAYING CHESS AFTER WATCHING THE OPPONENT'S OPENINGS."

Brazil conceded just one goal in six matches en route to the title—proof that samba could wear a tailored suit when necessary.

The Resistance: Coaches and Players Push Back

Yet not everyone embraces total quantification.

- **Dani Alves** openly mocked fitness graphs during warm-ups, saying, "I PREFER MY HEART TO TELL ME WHEN TO RUN."

- **Gabriel Jesus** admitted he found heat maps "boring" compared to the adrenaline of actual play.

- **Tite** balanced technology with humanism, ordering analysts to limit screen-time sessions to 20 minutes: "LET THE PLAYERS DREAM MORE THAN THEY CALCULATE."

There's a growing recognition: numbers are tools, not truths. Instinct, intuition, improvisation still reign supreme at the moment of the unpredictable.

The Next Frontiers: AI Coaches and Neuro-Tracking

Looking ahead, CBF's innovation department explores:

- **Neurocognitive Testing**: Measuring reaction times, decision-making under simulated match pressure.

- **VR Tactical Rehearsals**: Allowing players to "walk through" attacking patterns in headset simulations.

- **AI Tactical Assistants**: Predicting optimal substitution timings based on player workload, tactical shape shifts, and opponent vulnerabilities.

Already, Neymar's rehab programs at PSG include neural reaction drills tied to VR gameplay. Vinícius Júnior's off-season training features machine-learning feedback loops for shot selection.

The lines between athlete, analyst, and algorithm blur faster every year.

Epilogue: The Ball Still Has the Last Word

Inside CBF's high-tech command center, blinking dashboards predict probabilities: 74% chance of winning possession here, 68% chance of a through ball succeeding there.

But outside, on the grass, Neymar scoops a ball over two defenders. Vinícius backheels blind into space where he FEELS a run will come. A thirteen-year-old at a futsal court in Recife juggles a flattened ball between shoulder and ankle, dreaming not of algorithms, but of applause.

Data can plot movement. It cannot plot magic.

Brazil, wiser now, understands: spreadsheets guide the compass. But the dance? The dance still belongs to the soul.

Chapter 26   From Street Pitch to Twitch Stream: Digital Globalization of Style

At sunset in Rio's Cinelândia Square, a teenager juggles a ball while balancing it on his neck, toes tapping to an invisible beat. A small crowd gathers, smartphones aloft. Thirty seconds later, he flips the ball over his shoulder, snaps a rainbow flick into a spinning elastico, and ends with a cartwheel. The crowd roars. The video uploads within minutes. By nightfall, it racks up 20,000 views on TikTok and Instagram. By morning, a sportswear brand reposts it to three million followers.

This is football in the age of screens: freestylers, tricksters, e-sports stars, and social-media savants broadcasting the spirit of GINGA to the planet at WiFi speed. What once passed from alley to alley now uploads, hashtags, and monetizes across continents.

Brazil's magical style—born on concrete and sand—is no longer just a street art. It is a global currency, a brand, a live-streamed ecosystem where culture, commerce, and community collide.

From Streets to Screens: The Rise of the Digital Playground

Until the early 2000s, Brazil's footballing tricks were shared mainly by word-of-mouth, improvised in schoolyards or beaches, kept alive through local heroes and whispered legends.

But with the explosion of platforms like YouTube (launched 2005), Instagram (2010), TikTok (2016), and Twitch (2011), mastery could now skip physical borders. A teenager in Recife could post a nutmeg compilation that a freestyler in London would imitate hours later.

Early Brazilian YouTubers like **Séan Garnier**, **Freekickerz**, and local prodigies like **Adonias Fonseca** brought futsal footwork to global audiences. Videos of elasticos, no-look flicks, panna megs, and shoulder rolls clocked millions of plays. Tutorials democratized knowledge: no longer did you need a mentor at a dusty field; you needed a WiFi signal and imagination.

WHERE GARRINCHA ONCE WHISPERED TRICKS, NOW TUTORIALS SHOUTED.

The New Icons: Influencers as Football Ambassadors

Alongside traditional stars like Neymar and Vinícius Júnior, a new generation of football influencers rose—not through professional clubs, but through clicks:

- **Raquel Freestyle**: Brazilian freestyle queen with jaw-dropping trick compilations, brand deals with Adidas, and global choreography gigs.

- **Adonias Freestyle**: From favelas to Instagram stardom, pioneering the "flip tricks" popular across TikTok.

- **F2 Freestylers**: Not Brazilian, but inspired heavily by Brazilian futsal, blending carnival showmanship into their viral challenges.

These influencers built audiences not just by dazzling feet but by offering PERSONAL NARRATIVES: overcoming poverty, training in favelas, refusing gatekeeping traditions.

Samba-style football wasn't just on TV anymore. It was on your phone, your For You page, your feed—always one scroll away.

Freestyle vs. Professionalism: Two Worlds, One Ball

The explosion of freestyling triggered philosophical debates:

- **Is freestyle football "real" football?**

- **Does trick culture dilute the tactical and competitive integrity of the traditional game?**

- **Or does it refresh football's soul, reminding the world of play's primacy?**

Purists like former Brazil coach Carlos Alberto Parreira grumbled: "THERE ARE NO POINTS FOR ELASTICO. WE NEED GOALS, NOT GESTURES."

But others, like Neymar himself, defended trick culture: "BEFORE YOU SCORE, YOU HAVE TO DREAM. TRICKS ARE DREAMING."

In practice, the border blurred: clubs like PSG, Ajax, and even São Paulo FC incorporated freestyle drills into youth sessions to encourage creative body control and ball mastery under pressure.

The lesson: dribble tricks taught on TikTok often ended up as match-winning moves on Sunday.

E-Sports and Virtual Football: A New Battlefield

Parallel to freestyle's physical explosion came a virtual wave: FIFA video games, mobile apps, e-sports tournaments.

Brazilian gamers like **Fifilza** and **Zezinho** rose to global prominence, dazzling on virtual pitches. Twitch streams of FIFA matches garnered tens of thousands of concurrent viewers. Street skills morphed into joystick choreography.

Interestingly, e-sports reinforced Brazil's reputation for flair. In-game styles mimicked real-life panache: rainbow flicks, roulette spins, "samba passes" coded directly into game physics.

Young players no longer merely trained their bodies—they trained their thumbs, building virtual versions of GINGA pixel by pixel.

In the digital arena, a no-look through-ball scored as many likes as a real-world elastico.

The Brandification of Style: Samba as Commodity

Corporations moved swiftly.

Nike's JogaTV network, Adidas' Tango Squad campaigns, Puma's "Futuro" line—all commodified street football's aesthetics.

Social media amplified not just players but products:

- Signature boots designed for "street control" with hexagonal soles.

- "Favelas to the World" capsule clothing lines celebrating Brazilian urban culture.

- Brand-sponsored trick challenges ·offering prize money and academy scholarships.

For many freestylers and influencers, this meant unprecedented opportunity—but also delicate negotiations. How to stay authentic while surfing the commerce wave? How to honor GINGA without selling it too cheaply?

The best navigated it with grace, blending sponsorships with storytelling—showing both the sparkle and the sweat behind the scenes.

Democratization vs. Homogenization

There's a bittersweet undercurrent to globalization.

- **Good**: A kid in Nigeria can learn a sambadinha dribble from a kid in Recife in minutes.

- **Bad**: As styles go viral, individuality sometimes flattens into repetition—everyone chasing the same TikTok trends, the same moves.

Where GINGA once grew from chaotic improvisation, today's risk is algorithmic echo chambers: tricks designed more for virality than for soul.

Coaches caution young players not to learn only for clicks, but to explore new variations—to remember that Brazilian football flourished not from mimicry but from invention.

The challenge is clear: use the new tools, but stay true to the old spirit.

Epilogue: A Ball in Two Worlds

Tonight, in a narrow alley in Salvador, a boy balances a ball on his head while his friend livestreams on Instagram. A thousand miles away, a girl in Manchester replicates the move on her futsal team's TikTok channel. In Paris, a freestyler in Neymar's jersey performs a no-look elastico for a YouTube short.

The ball spins faster than ever, across asphalt and algorithms.

Brazil's gift to the world—a way of moving, dreaming, daring—now dances inside servers and streets alike.

In the age of Twitch streams and TikTok swipes, GINGA survives. It adapts. It uploads. It lives.

Because even behind a screen, a flick, a feint, a dribble still whispers the same invitation: play.

Chapter 27   The Soundtrack of Victory: Music, Dance, and Celebration Rituals

It's three minutes after full-time at the Maracanã, and the locker room already throbs like a rolling street party. Flip-flops slap tile floors in rhythm. A Bluetooth speaker blasts funk carioca beats so loud the air seems to shimmer. Neymar backheels a Gatorade bottle into a trash can while singing. Vinícius Júnior leads a half-sung, half-shouted chorus. Casemiro, usually stone-faced on the pitch, breaks into a swaying, shoulder-rolling forró step.

Victory in Brazil is never just a final whistle. It's an explosion of rhythm—music, dance, chant—that fuses sport to celebration. Samba-enredo, funk carioca, pagode, axé, forró: these are not background noises. They are fuel. They lubricate performance, relieve pressure, and broadcast joy to every corner of the stadium and screen.

In Brazil, football without music is like a carnival without drums—a party waiting to happen but unable to find its heartbeat.

The Locker Room as Drum Circle

Across generations, the Seleção's locker room has been a mobile sound system:

- 1970s: Samba-enredos from Rio's top samba schools played from battered cassette decks.

- 1990s: Pagode groups like Só Pra Contrariar dominated pre-match playlists.

- 2010s: Funk carioca—raw, bass-heavy, and explicit—became the dominant pulse.

- 2020s: A fusion: drill beats, gospel, trap, and old-school samba collide in glorious noise.

Before the 2002 World Cup final against Germany, players led by Cafu and Ronaldinho danced a mini-samba circle minutes before kick-off. In 2019's Copa América, Dani Alves curated a locker-room playlist blending vintage Tim Maia with MC Kevinho's urban anthems.

"Music makes the blood light," Dani Alves told ESPN. "You need to dance before you fight."

The Songs That Became Anthems

Certain tracks transcend the locker room to become part of the Seleção's public mythology:

- **"Na Cadência do Samba"** (Zé Keti): The unofficial soundtrack of the 1970 World Cup triumph.

- **"É Tetra!"** (Jorge Ben Jor): The rallying cry after Brazil's 1994 World Cup win, with Romário and Bebeto chanting it on live TV.

- **"Rap da Felicidade"** (Cidinho and Doca): A favela anthem that echoed through the 2002 locker rooms.

- **"Tá Rocando"** (MC Kevinho): Neymar and company's 2018 warm-up jam.

Music acts like an emotional memory bank. A goal celebration backed by a familiar beat becomes indelible. Years later, fans hear the song and time-travel back to the moment—Cafu kissing his captain's armband, Ronaldo flashing his gap-toothed smile, Marta crying tears of gold.

Funk Carioca and the Funkification of Football

Funk carioca, born in Rio's favelas, became the street anthem of Brazilian youth in the 2000s: aggressive, celebratory, explicitly local.

By the 2014 and 2018 World Cups, it dominated Seleção celebrations:

- Gabriel Jesus pantomiming funk moves after goals.

- Richarlison doing his viral "pombo" (pigeon) dance to a funk beat after scoring in Qatar 2022.

- Locker rooms turning into spontaneous funk battles with players like Paquetá leading the moves.

Musicologists point out that funk's improvisational nature mirrors street football: both reward spontaneity, rhythm shifts, cheeky moves.

Sociologist Hermano Vianna notes: "FUNK AND FOOTBALL BOTH WEAPONIZE JOY AGAINST PRECARITY."

The Dance Behind the Goal: Ritualized Improvisation

Post-goal celebrations in Brazil have evolved from simple fist pumps to choreographed spectacles:

- Bebeto's "baby rock" in 1994—cradling an imaginary newborn—after his son's birth.

- The 2002 squad's group samba after Rivaldo's goals.

- Neymar's Fortnite-inspired dances in 2018, blending gaming culture with field flair.

- Richarlison's 2022 "Dança do Pombo" spawning TikTok trends worldwide.

Far from trivial, these celebrations carry layered meaning:

- **Group dances** strengthen team identity.

- **Stylized rituals** reduce pressure by shifting focus onto communal joy.

- **Personal dances** brand players' personalities—Vinícius's samba steps, Antony's spinning celebrations.

In sports psychology, these expressions are recognized as "RHYTHMIC ANCHORS": physical rituals that reset adrenaline spikes and re-center emotional equilibrium.

Choreographers and Psychologists Behind the Scenes

At the elite level, dance is no accident. Brazil's national squads have quietly incorporated movement coaches and musical consultants into training:

- Pre-tournament sessions include coordinated movement drills blending samba, capoeira, and funk carioca.

- Players choose their goal celebration songs during camp, fostering emotional attachment.

- Choreographers like Deborah Colker have consulted on pre-match rituals, promoting rhythmic flow states.

Psychologist Regina Brandão, long associated with the Seleção, explains: "RHYTHM IS ANCESTRAL. IT PULLS ATHLETES OUT OF OVERTHINKING AND INTO EMBODIED CONFIDENCE."

When players sway together before a penalty shootout, they synchronize heart rates, breathing patterns, and emotional tempo. Dance becomes invisible armor.

When Songs Heal Defeats

Music doesn't just crown victories. It helps mend defeats.

After the 7–1 Mineirão collapse in 2014, players gathered in the locker room. Silence reigned—until a massage therapist played "Tente Outra Vez" ("Try Again") by Raul Seixas on a small speaker.

Several players, including Júlio César, later said that hearing that song broke the paralysis. They cried. Then they began the slow walk back toward national forgiveness.

After the 2022 World Cup loss to Croatia, it was the old sambas that filtered through the Seleção hotel corridors, softer, slower—songs of resilience rather than triumph.

Brazil sings in joy. Brazil sings in sorrow. Always.

The Fans' Soundtrack: Drums, Choruses, and Portable Carnivals

Fans amplify the soundtrack on matchdays:

- **Baterias** (drum corps) create layered polyrhythms echoing samba school traditions.

- **Mosaicos Cantados**—singing mosaics—where entire stands perform coordinated songs with colored cards and call-and-response refrains.

- **Portable sound systems** wheeled into stadium parking lots blast funk, samba, and pagode, creating pre-match street carnivals.

Songs morph by the minute: political critiques, praise for heroes, savage banter for rivals. Every major city has local variations, with Rio's funk basslines dominating urban centers and Recife's forró rhythms coloring the Northeast.

Brazil's football fandom is not silent support. It is sonic siege.

Epilogue: The Unwritten Score

There's no coaching manual for the soundtrack of victory. No analytics dashboard can measure its impact.

But when you see Neymar samba-shuffling after a goal, when you hear a thousand drums booming in the Morumbi rafters, when you feel a locker room pulsing like a living heart—then you understand: rhythm is not decoration.

It is propulsion. It is celebration. It is survival.

In Brazil, the ball dances. So must the heart.

Chapter 28 Fields of Tomorrow: Sustainability, Inclusion, and Social Impact

Under a neon sunset in São Paulo's Paraisópolis favela, where high-rises loom like watchtowers, a cluster of children chase a ball across an improvised rooftop pitch. The turf is synthetic, made from recycled plastic. Solar panels line the perimeter. LEDs flicker on, powered by the day's harvest. No parents can afford tickets to the Morumbi or Maracanã, but up here, among laundry lines and corrugated iron, the JOGO BONITO beats stronger than ever.

This is Brazilian football's future—not just played but rebuilt, reimagined. Beyond the glare of World Cup stadiums and billion-dollar transfers, grassroots movements, NGOs, and forward-thinking clubs are turning football into an engine for environmental change, social justice, and inclusive growth.

The fields of tomorrow will not simply entertain. They will sustain. They will educate. They will heal.

Solar Pitches and Recycled Dreams

Across Brazil's urban landscapes, rooftop and micro-pitches have proliferated. NGOs like **Love.Fútbol** and **Gol de Letra** (founded by ex-players Raí and Leonardo) champion sustainable facilities:

- **Solar-Powered Lighting**: Fields in Recife, Rio, and Brasília now use photovoltaic panels to power evening matches, cutting energy costs by up to 70%.

- **Recycled Materials**: Old tires become artificial turf; discarded plastics morph into goalposts and benches.

- **Rainwater Collection Systems**: Pitches in drought-prone areas like the Sertão reuse rainfall to maintain grass fields without draining city water supplies.

In 2019, a groundbreaking "eco-pitch" opened in Curitiba, using kinetic tiles that generate electricity from players' footfall—a literal example of play fueling light.

Football pitches are no longer environmental burdens. They are becoming small power plants of joy.

Football Against Racism: A Continual Fight

Brazil's myth of racial democracy—where football supposedly united all colors—has long been challenged by reality. Black players like Pelé, Romário, and Vinícius Júnior faced (and still face) racial abuse from crowds, media, and officials.

Modern initiatives tackle this head-on:

- **CBF's Zero Tolerance Policy**: Matches can now be suspended if racist abuse occurs, with stadium bans for offending fans.

- **Campaigns like "Respeita Meu Cabelo, Respeita Minha Cor"** ("Respect My Hair, Respect My Color") run at all league levels, celebrating Afro-Brazilian identity.

- **Player-Led Protests**: In 2023, Vinícius Júnior led La Liga walkouts, inspiring Brazilian players to show solidarity by raising black power fists before domestic matches.

At grassroots levels, community clubs host workshops intertwining football training with Black consciousness education, using the ball not just to dribble—but to liberate.

As sociologist Silvio Almeida puts it: "EVERY STEP ON THE BALL IS A STEP AGAINST RACISM."

Gender Inclusion: Beyond the Boys' Club

After decades of neglect, women's football in Brazil is no longer an afterthought.

- **CBF Mandate**: Since 2019, all professional men's clubs must maintain a women's team to compete in national competitions.

- **Investment in Grassroots Girls' Programs**: NGOs like PROJETO MENINAS EM CAMPO ("Girls on the Field Project") transform abandoned lots into safe training spaces.

- **Rising Role Models**: Marta's legacy has ignited a new wave of young talents like Ary Borges and Debinha, visible on billboards, ads, and FIFA games.

Locker rooms, once exclusively male sanctuaries, now share walls with girls plotting their own bicycle kicks and panenkas.

In Belo Horizonte, an annual "Samba Girls' Cup" fuses futsal, music, and female empowerment—proving that the GINGA knows no gender.

Literacy Under the Bleachers: Football as School

Underneath the bleachers of Flamengo's Gávea training ground, and under temporary tents in Salvador's community fields, a quiet revolution grows: literacy classes for children who come to play, but stay to learn.

Programs like **Futebol e Letras** ("Football and Letters") connect reading to football:

- Children write match reports of their own games.

- Math skills are honed by calculating player stats.

- History lessons include the lives of pioneers like Leônidas da Silva and Marta.

As coach and educator Silvana Souza notes: "THE BALL HOOKS THE HEART. THEN WE HOOK THE MIND."

By embedding literacy into leisure, Brazil combats one of its most persistent inequalities.

Environmental Innovation at the Club Level

Top clubs have also joined the sustainability push:

- **Palmeiras**: Allianz Parque boasts a state-of-the-art rainwater capture system, recycling 75% of stadium water usage.

- **Atlético Paranaense**: Arena da Baixada achieved FIFA's first Green Building Certification in Latin America.

- **Grêmio**: The club launched carbon offset programs, planting trees for each home match played.

Even team jerseys tell the story: Corinthians and Fluminense have worn kits made from recycled plastic bottles, blurring the line between style and sustainability.

Football's carbon footprint—still significant due to travel and construction—is slowly being recalibrated, one solar panel and one green roof at a time.

The Role of Technology: Apps, Crowdsourcing, and Smart Fields

Mobile apps allow grassroots coaches to track attendance, manage tournaments, and report maintenance issues on community pitches.

Smart fields equipped with moisture sensors, kinetic lights, and automated sprinkler systems dot cities like São Paulo and Fortaleza, reducing maintenance costs and environmental impact.

Even crowdsourced fundraising models—like VAQUINHAS (Brazilian GoFundMe equivalents)—help communities build pitches where city budgets fall short.

Where once a dusty lot awaited divine intervention, now a smartphone summons change.

The Challenges Ahead: Barriers That Remain

Despite progress, hurdles persist:

- **Access Inequality**: Rural regions, especially in the Amazon and Northeast, lag behind in facilities and opportunities.

- **Racism and Sexism**: Despite high-profile campaigns, incidents of abuse still mar games at all levels.

- **Commercial Pressure**: Mega-events often divert funding away from grassroots fields toward elite stadiums.

- **Environmental Costs**: Large club expansions risk environmental degradation without careful planning.

The dream is alive—but it demands vigilance, inclusion, and constant reinvention.

Epilogue: Planting the Ball, Planting the Future

Back in Paraisópolis, under solar lights and neon graffiti, a teenager feints past two defenders and rifles the ball into a net made from old fishing nets. Cheers ripple through the rooftop.

He points to the stars above the favela skyline—not just the literal stars, but the dreams they symbolize.

Tomorrow, he'll attend math classes run by volunteers who coach his team. Tomorrow, he'll help water the rooftop garden planted next to the pitch. Tomorrow, he'll play again—on a field powered by sunshine and stubborn hope.

In Brazil, the ball keeps rolling. But now it rolls greener, smarter, fairer.

The JOGO BONITO survives not just because it enchants—but because it adapts, includes, and insists that the future must dance along with it.

Epilogue – Eterno Jogo

The sun hangs low over Ipanema, a blood-orange disk melting into the Atlantic. Barefoot kids chase each other along the damp sand, juggling whatever they can find—half-deflated balls, plastic bottles, even clumps of driftwood. They call fouls with grins. They argue goals with passion. They invent rules, break them, and invent again.

No scouts watch. No cameras roll. No metrics are gathered. Only the endless rhythm of foot to ball to sky.

After all the World Cups and golden boots, after the drone-footage training sessions and TikTok celebrations, it still begins here—on beaches and alleys and rooftop pitches where creativity is currency and laughter is law.

Brazil's century-long football odyssey has given the world more than goals and trophies. It gave a philosophy: that football, at its purest, is an act of joy. That improvisation can triumph over brute force. That rhythm and daring still matter as much as systems and spreadsheets.

Across these pages, we've seen how Brazil spun a colonial import into a cultural epic:
From Charles Miller's stitched balls to Marta's golden tears;
From Garrincha's crooked dribbles to Richarlison's pigeon dance;
From the concrete colosseums to solar-lit favelas in the sky.

We saw dreams battered by dictatorship, commodified by marketing, stretched across Twitch streams, but never extinguished.

The ball kept moving, and with it, so did Brazil's heartbeat—syncopated, unpredictable, eternal.

Other nations have risen. New empires have flexed their tactical muscles. But when a five-year-old somewhere in Africa juggles a ball with a smile, when a teenager in Europe tries a rainbow flick in a concrete court, they are—whether they know it or not—tapping into a current sparked on Brazilian streets.

The world may chart football's future with algorithms and balance sheets, but it will still measure greatness by moments born of audacity, of rhythm, of soul.

And nowhere has that pulse beaten stronger, longer, or more beautifully than here.

Back on the beach, the sky deepens into indigo. The kids play until the light disappears, and even then, they don't stop. They invent new games under the stars.

The ball spins into the night, weightless.

The JOGO BONITO lives on.

Eterno.

Forever.

Appendix A — Key Player Biographies

Pelé (Edson Arantes do Nascimento)
Born: October 23, 1940 — Três Corações, Minas Gerais
Position: Forward

Often called "The King" (O REI), Pelé embodied the spirit of JOGO BONITO like no other. A three-time World Cup winner (1958, 1962, 1970), he blended dazzling footwork, extraordinary vision, and clinical finishing. Off the pitch, Pelé became Brazil's first global sporting ambassador, symbolizing football's power to transcend race, politics, and borders. His career, spanning Santos FC and the New York Cosmos, remains the gold standard of greatness.

Garrincha (Manuel Francisco dos Santos)
Born: October 28, 1933 — Pau Grande, Rio de Janeiro
Position: Winger

Bow-legged and blessed with unteachable improvisation, Garrincha became Brazil's folk hero. Nicknamed "The Joy of the People" (ALEGRIA DO POVO), he led Brazil to the 1962 World Cup title after Pelé's injury, mesmerizing defenders with impossible dribbles. Off the field, his struggles with injury and personal demons made him a tragic, beloved figure— proof that genius often blooms from imperfection.

Sócrates (Sócrates Brasileiro Sampaio de Souza Vieira de Oliveira)
Born: February 19, 1954 — Belém de Pará
Position: Midfielder

Tall, cerebral, and politically fearless, Sócrates captained the romantic 1982 Seleção and became a global symbol of athlete activism through the Corinthians Democracy movement. A doctor by training and a revolutionary in spirit, he fused midfield elegance with a demand that football—and society—remain spaces for freedom.

Romário (Romário de Souza Faria)
Born: January 29, 1966 — Rio de Janeiro
Position: Striker

With unmatchable instinct and a predator's finish, Romário powered Brazil to its fourth World Cup title in 1994. Known for his lazy saunters and deadly strikes, he epitomized Brazilian football's gift for turning nonchalance into lethal artistry. After retiring, Romário entered politics, continuing to fight for marginalized communities.

Ronaldo (Ronaldo Luís Nazário de Lima)

Born: September 18, 1976 — Rio de Janeiro

Position: Striker

Dubbed "The Phenomenon" (O FENÔMENO), Ronaldo combined blistering pace, deceptive strength, and delicate touch. His redemption arc—from injury devastation to Golden Boot winner at the 2002 World Cup—etched him into Brazil's national lore. Clubs like Barcelona, Inter Milan, and Real Madrid witnessed his dazzling powers at their height.

Ronaldinho (Ronaldo de Assis Moreira)

Born: March 21, 1980 — Porto Alegre

Position: Attacking Midfielder / Forward

With his trademark toothy grin and elastic creativity, Ronaldinho brought pure playfulness back to the global stage. World Cup winner in 2002 and FIFA World Player of the Year twice, he blurred the lines between footballer and entertainer. Ronaldinho's joy on the ball reminded the world why Brazil remains football's beating heart.

Marta (Marta Vieira da Silva)
Born: February 19, 1986 — Dois Riachos, Alagoas
Position: Forward

Widely considered the greatest female footballer of all time, Marta won a record six FIFA World Player of the Year awards. Her dazzling runs, lethal left foot, and relentless spirit made her a global icon. More than just a player, Marta opened doors for generations of girls dreaming of the pitch.

Neymar Jr. (Neymar da Silva Santos Júnior)
Born: February 5, 1992 — Mogi das Cruzes, São Paulo
Position: Forward

Neymar's elastic dribbles, audacious flicks, and instinct for spectacle made him Brazil's most recognizable star of the modern era. His journey—from Santos prodigy to Barcelona magician to PSG phenomenon—traced both the opportunities and burdens of 21st-century fame. Love him or loathe him, Neymar carries Brazil's footballing hopes into each new cycle.

Vinícius Júnior (Vinícius José Paixão de Oliveira Júnior)
Born: July 12, 2000 — São Gonçalo, Rio de Janeiro
Position: Winger

Electrifying with pace and fearless with the ball, Vinícius embodies the future of Brazilian flair. A Champions League winner with Real Madrid by age 21, his samba-infused footwork and celebratory dance moves mark a generation blending street football energy with elite discipline.

Richarlison (Richarlison de Andrade)
Born: May 10, 1997 — Nova Venécia, Espírito Santo
Position: Forward

Nicknamed O POMBO ("The Pigeon") for his trademark dance, Richarlison's journey from humble beginnings to Olympic gold and World Cup heroics shows grit beneath the showmanship. Equally capable of a cheeky flick or a bulldozing header, he personifies the enduring duality of Brazilian football: grace and grind.

Dani Alves (Daniel Alves da Silva)
Born: May 6, 1983 — Juazeiro, Bahia
Position: Right Back

One of the most decorated footballers in history, Dani Alves redefined the fullback role with relentless attacking surges, technical mastery, and locker-room leadership. His samba spirit flowed not only in his playing style but also in his fierce love for the AMARELINHA jersey.

Appendix B — Chronological Timeline of Major Events

1894

Charles Miller returns from England to São Paulo, bringing two footballs, a rulebook, and boundless enthusiasm. The first organized matches between Anglo-Brazilian social clubs spark the birth of Brazilian football.

1902

The inaugural **Campeonato Paulista** (São Paulo State Championship) is held, Brazil's first formal football competition.

1923

Vasco da Gama's multiracial squad wins the Rio de Janeiro championship, shattering racial and class barriers in the Brazilian game.

1938

At the World Cup in France, Leônidas da Silva, the "Rubber Man," dazzles Europe with his bicycle kicks and becomes the tournament's top scorer.

1950

Brazil hosts its first World Cup. In the newly built Maracanã Stadium, Uruguay stuns Brazil 2–1 in the final (MARACANAZO), triggering a national trauma.

1958

A 17-year-old Pelé bursts onto the world stage, helping Brazil win its first World Cup in Sweden. The JOGO BONITO is officially born.

1962

Despite Pelé's early injury, Garrincha carries Brazil to a second consecutive World Cup title in Chile, further embedding flair as the national style.

1970

Brazil wins its third World Cup in Mexico, led by Pelé, Jairzinho, Tostão, Rivellino, and Carlos Alberto. The team's mesmerizing style, broadcast in color television worldwide, cements Brazil as football's spiritual homeland.

1982

Tele Santana's romantic squad, featuring Sócrates, Zico, and Falcão, enthralls the world at the Spain World Cup but falls to Italy. Beauty is celebrated even in defeat.

1994

Brazil wins its fourth World Cup in the USA, ending a 24-year drought. Romário and Bebeto lead a pragmatic but effective side to glory via a dramatic penalty shootout.

1998

Brazil reaches the World Cup final but falls 3–0 to France. The mysterious pre-match collapse of star Ronaldo remains one of football's great unsolved dramas.

2002

Ronaldo's redemption arc is completed as Brazil wins its fifth World Cup in South Korea and Japan. Ronaldo, Rivaldo, and Ronaldinho form a fearsome attacking trident.

2007

Marta leads Brazil's women's national team to the FIFA Women's World Cup final, dazzling with individual brilliance and helping to globalize women's football in Brazil.

2014
Brazil hosts the World Cup but suffers a catastrophic 7–1 semifinal defeat to Germany in Belo Horizonte—the **Mineiraço**—sparking a national reckoning.

2016
At the Rio Olympics, Brazil's men's team, captained by Neymar, finally wins its first Olympic gold medal, defeating Germany on penalties at the Maracanã Stadium.

2019
Brazil wins the Copa América on home soil under Tite, with a disciplined and refreshed squad. The victory signals a new, balanced tactical era.

2022
Brazil dazzles at the Qatar World Cup with flair and youth but exits in the quarterfinals after a dramatic penalty shootout loss to Croatia. Richarlison's pigeon dance becomes a viral symbol of joy despite heartbreak.

2023

Vinícius Júnior leads player-driven anti-racism protests after facing abuse in Spain, igniting global solidarity movements across football.

2024

Brazilian grassroots football surges ahead with sustainable pitches, inclusive youth programs, and a new generation blending street flair with digital savviness, ensuring that the spirit of JOGO BONITO remains vibrant for the next century.

Appendix C — Tactical Glossary

Ginga

The quintessential Brazilian way of moving with the ball, blending sway, feint, rhythm, and improvisation. GINGA is more than a dribble—it's an embodied dance, a physical expression of unpredictability and joy.

Jogo Bonito (THE BEAUTIFUL GAME)

A romantic ideal of football emphasizing creativity, flair, fair play, and attacking artistry. Though associated globally with Brazil, the phrase was popularized in part by Nike marketing campaigns in the 1990s.

4-2-4 Formation

A revolutionary attacking system, pioneered by Brazil in the 1958 World Cup, deploying four defenders, two midfielders, and four forwards. It blended European structure with Brazilian attacking exuberance, laying the foundation for future tactical evolution.

Positional Play (POSICIONAMENTO)

The modern principle of structuring player movement around creating space, overloads, and numerical superiority. In Brazil's newer generations under Tite and beyond, POSICIONAMENTO married samba freedom with tactical discipline.

Garra

A Portuguese term meaning grit, determination, and mental toughness. In Brazilian football, GARRA complements GINGA— the steel behind the style, especially celebrated during hard-fought matches.

Pressão Alta (HIGH PRESS)

Tactical system where teams aggressively close down opponents high up the field to win back possession early. Once rare in Brazil's traditionally more patient game, it became crucial in the post-2014 tactical shift.

Pivô

In futsal and youth development, the PIVÔ is the attacking reference point (pivot), playing with the back to goal, linking play and creating space. Many Brazilian forwards learn their trade first as PIVÔS in tight indoor courts.

Elastic Dribble (ELASTICO)

A rapid, deceptive dribble where the player pushes the ball outward before snapping it back inward in a single fluid motion, famously used by Rivellino and Ronaldinho. A signature of Brazilian street flair.

Linha Alta (HIGH DEFENSIVE LINE)

A strategy where defenders position themselves further upfield to compress the opponent's space and enable aggressive pressing. Risky if mistimed, but crucial for modern Brazilian defensive strategies post-2010.

Sambadinha

An informal term for goal celebrations or dribbles that mimic samba dance steps. When players like Vinícius Júnior celebrate with SAMBADINHA, they honor Brazil's fusion of dance and football culture.

Desarme

The act of dispossessing an opponent cleanly, crucial for defensive midfielders. Players like Casemiro have turned DESARMES into an art form, combining aggression with precision.

Paredinha

A quick wall-pass (give-and-go), often executed in futsal and tight spaces. The paredinha is essential for breaking defensive lines with one-touch brilliance.

Jogada Ensaiada (SET PIECE PLAY)

A pre-rehearsed set-piece routine, often involving misdirection and coordinated movement. Brazil's tactical evolution increasingly relied on JOGADAS ENSAIADAS to surprise tightly organized defenses.

Saída de Bola (BALL EXIT)

The orchestration of building play from the back, starting with goalkeepers and defenders under pressure. A major focus for Brazil's tactical modernization post-2014.

Dança do Pombo (PIGEON DANCE)

Richarlison's viral celebration, characterized by bouncing shoulder movements imitating a pigeon. It became an emblem of joy during Brazil's 2022 World Cup run.

Tabelinha

The classic Brazilian one-two pass, typically rapid and used to split defenders. In countless pickup games, TABELINHAS are the fastest way to slice open even crowded defenses.

Roda de Bola (BALL CIRCLE)

Training exercise where players form a circle and keep the ball airborne using all parts of the body. Beyond conditioning, it emphasizes ball control, creativity, and group rhythm.

Appendix D — World Cup Statistics

Brazil's Overall World Cup Record (as of 2022)

- **Appearances**: 22 (Every tournament since 1930 except 1950, when they hosted, and every edition afterward)

- **Titles**: 5 (1958, 1962, 1970, 1994, 2002)

- **Finals Played**: 7 (Winners in 5, Runners-up in 1950 and 1998)

- **Semi-finals Reached**: 11 times

- **Total Matches Played**: 114

- **Wins**: 76

- **Draws**: 20

- **Losses**: 18

- **Goals Scored**: 237

- **Goals Conceded**: 128

Titles by Year

- **1958 — Sweden**
  Champions (Pelé, Vavá, Garrincha lead Brazil's first title)

- **1962 — Chile**
  Champions (Garrincha shines as Pelé is injured)

- **1970 — Mexico**
  Champions (Pelé's third title, Carlos Alberto's legendary goal)

- **1994 — USA**
  Champions (Romário and Bebeto star, Brazil wins on penalties)

- **2002 — South Korea & Japan**
  Champions (Ronaldo's redemption, Rivaldo and Ronaldinho magic)

Finals Reached

- 1950 — Runner-up (Lost 1–2 to Uruguay, MARACANAZO)

- 1958 — Champions (Beat Sweden 5–2)

- 1962 — Champions (Beat Czechoslovakia 3–1)

- 1970 — Champions (Beat Italy 4–1)

- 1994 — Champions (Beat Italy 0–0, 3–2 on penalties)

- 1998 — Runner-up (Lost 0–3 to France)

- 2002 — Champions (Beat Germany 2–0)

Top Brazilian World Cup Goal Scorers

- **Ronaldo**: 15 goals (1998, 2002, 2006)

- **Pelé**: 12 goals (1958, 1962, 1966, 1970)

- **Neymar**: 8 goals (2014, 2018, 2022)

- **Vavá**: 9 goals (1958, 1962)

- **Jairzinho**: 7 goals (1970 — scored in every match)

Most World Cup Appearances by Brazilian Players

- **Cafu**: 20 matches (1994, 1998, 2002, 2006)

- **Ronaldo**: 19 matches

- **Thiago Silva**: 18 matches (2010, 2014, 2018, 2022)

- **Djalma Santos**: 16 matches (1954, 1958, 1962, 1966)

- **Pelé**: 14 matches

Notable Records

- **Most World Cup Titles**: Brazil (5) — the only nation to achieve this milestone.

- **First Team to Win Three World Cups**: 1970 — Pelé lifting the Jules Rimet Trophy permanently for Brazil.

- **First Nation to Win a World Cup Outside Its Home Continent**: Brazil (1958, Europe — Sweden).

- **Only Team to Appear at Every World Cup**: Brazil (1930–2022, no missed editions).

- **Longest World Cup Winning Streak**: 11 consecutive matches (2002 to 2006).

Notable Low Points

- **1950**: MARACANAZO — Shock defeat to Uruguay in Rio, despite overwhelming expectations.

- **1966**: Group-stage exit in England — Pelé injured and fouled mercilessly.

- **1982**: Defeat to Italy in Spain, despite dazzling displays of attacking football.

- **2014**: MINEIRAÇO — 1–7 semifinal loss to Germany on home soil, the worst defeat in Brazil's history.

Recent World Cup Results

- **2014 (Brazil)**: Fourth Place (Lost 1–7 to Germany in Semifinal, 0–3 to Netherlands in Third-Place Match)

- **2018 (Russia)**: Quarterfinal Exit (Lost 1–2 to Belgium)

- **2022 (Qatar)**: Quarterfinal Exit (Lost to Croatia on penalties after 1–1 draw)

www.ingramcontent.com/pod-product-compliance
Ingram Content Group UK Ltd.
Pitfield, Milton Keynes, MK11 3LW, UK
UKHW051850181125
9046UKWH00008B/31

9 781923 504622